C-3402   **CAREER EXAMINATION SERIES**

*This is your
PASSBOOK for...*

Police Operations Aide

*Test Preparation Study Guide
Questions & Answers*

COPYRIGHT NOTICE

This book is SOLELY intended for, is sold ONLY to, and its use is RESTRICTED to individual, bona fide applicants or candidates who qualify by virtue of having seriously filed applications for appropriate license, certificate, professional and/or promotional advancement, higher school matriculation, scholarship, or other legitimate requirements of education and/or governmental authorities.

This book is NOT intended for use, class instruction, tutoring, training, duplication, copying, reprinting, excerption, or adaptation, etc., by:

1) Other publishers
2) Proprietors and/or Instructors of "Coaching" and/or Preparatory Courses
3) Personnel and/or Training Divisions of commercial, industrial, and governmental organizations
4) Schools, colleges, or universities and/or their departments and staffs, including teachers and other personnel
5) Testing Agencies or Bureaus
6) Study groups which seek by the purchase of a single volume to copy and/or duplicate and/or adapt this material for use by the group as a whole without having purchased individual volumes for each of the members of the group
7) Et al.

Such persons would be in violation of appropriate Federal and State statutes.

PROVISION OF LICENSING AGREEMENTS – Recognized educational, commercial, industrial, and governmental institutions and organizations, and others legitimately engaged in educational pursuits, including training, testing, and measurement activities, may address request for a licensing agreement to the copyright owners, who will determine whether, and under what conditions, including fees and charges, the materials in this book may be used them. In other words, a licensing facility exists for the legitimate use of the material in this book on other than an individual basis. However, it is asseverated and affirmed here that the material in this book CANNOT be used without the receipt of the express permission of such a licensing agreement from the Publishers. Inquiries re licensing should be addressed to the company, attention rights and permissions department.

All rights reserved, including the right of reproduction in whole or in part, in any form or by any means, electronic or mechanical, including photocopying, recording, or by any information storage and retrieval system, without permission in writing from the Publisher.

Copyright © 2024 by
National Learning Corporation

212 Michael Drive, Syosset, NY 11791
(516) 921-8888 • www.passbooks.com
E-mail: info@passbooks.com

PASSBOOK® SERIES

THE *PASSBOOK® SERIES* has been created to prepare applicants and candidates for the ultimate academic battlefield – the examination room.

At some time in our lives, each and every one of us may be required to take an examination – for validation, matriculation, admission, qualification, registration, certification, or licensure.

Based on the assumption that every applicant or candidate has met the basic formal educational standards, has taken the required number of courses, and read the necessary texts, the *PASSBOOK® SERIES* furnishes the one special preparation which may assure passing with confidence, instead of failing with insecurity. Examination questions – together with answers – are furnished as the basic vehicle for study so that the mysteries of the examination and its compounding difficulties may be eliminated or diminished by a sure method.

This book is meant to help you pass your examination provided that you qualify and are serious in your objective.

The entire field is reviewed through the huge store of content information which is succinctly presented through a provocative and challenging approach – the question-and-answer method.

A climate of success is established by furnishing the correct answers at the end of each test.

You soon learn to recognize types of questions, forms of questions, and patterns of questioning. You may even begin to anticipate expected outcomes.

You perceive that many questions are repeated or adapted so that you can gain acute insights, which may enable you to score many sure points.

You learn how to confront new questions, or types of questions, and to attack them confidently and work out the correct answers.

You note objectives and emphases, and recognize pitfalls and dangers, so that you may make positive educational adjustments.

Moreover, you are kept fully informed in relation to new concepts, methods, practices, and directions in the field.

You discover that you are actually taking the examination all the time: you are preparing for the examination by "taking" an examination, not by reading extraneous and/or supererogatory textbooks.

In short, this PASSBOOK®, used directedly, should be an important factor in helping you to pass your test.

POLICE OPERATIONS AIDE

DUTIES
Performs varied supportive clerical duties in a police precinct or headquarters. Types information for official police blotter, calls tow trucks, prepares reports, processes sealed records and assists in paper preparation for missing persons, arrests, etc. May operate a computer terminal, switchboard, radios and other electronic equipment and various business machines. The work is performed under the supervision of police staff members and is performed on a rotating basis. Performs related work as required.

SCOPE OF THE EXAMINATION
The <u>multiple-choice</u> test will cover knowledge, skills, and abilities in such areas as:
1. Understanding and interpreting written material;
2. Coding/decoding information;
3. Clerical operations with letters and numbers; and
4. Name and number checking.

HOW TO TAKE A TEST

I. YOU MUST PASS AN EXAMINATION

A. *WHAT EVERY CANDIDATE SHOULD KNOW*

Examination applicants often ask us for help in preparing for the written test. What can I study in advance? What kinds of questions will be asked? How will the test be given? How will the papers be graded?

As an applicant for a civil service examination, you may be wondering about some of these things. Our purpose here is to suggest effective methods of advance study and to describe civil service examinations.

Your chances for success on this examination can be increased if you know how to prepare. Those "pre-examination jitters" can be reduced if you know what to expect. You can even experience an adventure in good citizenship if you know why civil service exams are given.

B. *WHY ARE CIVIL SERVICE EXAMINATIONS GIVEN?*

Civil service examinations are important to you in two ways. As a citizen, you want public jobs filled by employees who know how to do their work. As a job seeker, you want a fair chance to compete for that job on an equal footing with other candidates. The best-known means of accomplishing this two-fold goal is the competitive examination.

Exams are widely publicized throughout the nation. They may be administered for jobs in federal, state, city, municipal, town or village governments or agencies.

Any citizen may apply, with some limitations, such as the age or residence of applicants. Your experience and education may be reviewed to see whether you meet the requirements for the particular examination. When these requirements exist, they are reasonable and applied consistently to all applicants. Thus, a competitive examination may cause you some uneasiness now, but it is your privilege and safeguard.

C. *HOW ARE CIVIL SERVICE EXAMS DEVELOPED?*

Examinations are carefully written by trained technicians who are specialists in the field known as "psychological measurement," in consultation with recognized authorities in the field of work that the test will cover. These experts recommend the subject matter areas or skills to be tested; only those knowledges or skills important to your success on the job are included. The most reliable books and source materials available are used as references. Together, the experts and technicians judge the difficulty level of the questions.

Test technicians know how to phrase questions so that the problem is clearly stated. Their ethics do not permit "trick" or "catch" questions. Questions may have been tried out on sample groups, or subjected to statistical analysis, to determine their usefulness.

Written tests are often used in combination with performance tests, ratings of training and experience, and oral interviews. All of these measures combine to form the best-known means of finding the right person for the right job.

II. HOW TO PASS THE WRITTEN TEST

A. NATURE OF THE EXAMINATION

To prepare intelligently for civil service examinations, you should know how they differ from school examinations you have taken. In school you were assigned certain definite pages to read or subjects to cover. The examination questions were quite detailed and usually emphasized memory. Civil service exams, on the other hand, try to discover your present ability to perform the duties of a position, plus your potentiality to learn these duties. In other words, a civil service exam attempts to predict how successful you will be. Questions cover such a broad area that they cannot be as minute and detailed as school exam questions.

In the public service similar kinds of work, or positions, are grouped together in one "class." This process is known as *position-classification*. All the positions in a class are paid according to the salary range for that class. One class title covers all of these positions, and they are all tested by the same examination.

B. FOUR BASIC STEPS

1) Study the announcement

How, then, can you know what subjects to study? Our best answer is: "Learn as much as possible about the class of positions for which you've applied." The exam will test the knowledge, skills and abilities needed to do the work.

Your most valuable source of information about the position you want is the official exam announcement. This announcement lists the training and experience qualifications. Check these standards and apply only if you come reasonably close to meeting them.

The brief description of the position in the examination announcement offers some clues to the subjects which will be tested. Think about the job itself. Review the duties in your mind. Can you perform them, or are there some in which you are rusty? Fill in the blank spots in your preparation.

Many jurisdictions preview the written test in the exam announcement by including a section called "Knowledge and Abilities Required," "Scope of the Examination," or some similar heading. Here you will find out specifically what fields will be tested.

2) Review your own background

Once you learn in general what the position is all about, and what you need to know to do the work, ask yourself which subjects you already know fairly well and which need improvement. You may wonder whether to concentrate on improving your strong areas or on building some background in your fields of weakness. When the announcement has specified "some knowledge" or "considerable knowledge," or has used adjectives like "beginning principles of…" or "advanced … methods," you can get a clue as to the number and difficulty of questions to be asked in any given field. More questions, and hence broader coverage, would be included for those subjects which are more important in the work. Now weigh your strengths and weaknesses against the job requirements and prepare accordingly.

3) Determine the level of the position

Another way to tell how intensively you should prepare is to understand the level of the job for which you are applying. Is it the entering level? In other words, is this the position in which beginners in a field of work are hired? Or is it an intermediate or advanced level? Sometimes this is indicated by such words as "Junior" or "Senior" in the class title. Other jurisdictions use Roman numerals to designate the level – Clerk I, Clerk II, for example. The word "Supervisor" sometimes appears in the title. If the level is not indicated by the title, check the description of duties. Will you be working under very close supervision, or will you have responsibility for independent decisions in this work?

4) Choose appropriate study materials

Now that you know the subjects to be examined and the relative amount of each subject to be covered, you can choose suitable study materials. For beginning level jobs, or even advanced ones, if you have a pronounced weakness in some aspect of your training, read a modern, standard textbook in that field. Be sure it is up to date and has general coverage. Such books are normally available at your library, and the librarian will be glad to help you locate one. For entry-level positions, questions of appropriate difficulty are chosen – neither highly advanced questions, nor those too simple. Such questions require careful thought but not advanced training.

If the position for which you are applying is technical or advanced, you will read more advanced, specialized material. If you are already familiar with the basic principles of your field, elementary textbooks would waste your time. Concentrate on advanced textbooks and technical periodicals. Think through the concepts and review difficult problems in your field.

These are all general sources. You can get more ideas on your own initiative, following these leads. For example, training manuals and publications of the government agency which employs workers in your field can be useful, particularly for technical and professional positions. A letter or visit to the government department involved may result in more specific study suggestions, and certainly will provide you with a more definite idea of the exact nature of the position you are seeking.

III. KINDS OF TESTS

Tests are used for purposes other than measuring knowledge and ability to perform specified duties. For some positions, it is equally important to test ability to make adjustments to new situations or to profit from training. In others, basic mental abilities not dependent on information are essential. Questions which test these things may not appear as pertinent to the duties of the position as those which test for knowledge and information. Yet they are often highly important parts of a fair examination. For very general questions, it is almost impossible to help you direct your study efforts. What we can do is to point out some of the more common of these general abilities needed in public service positions and describe some typical questions.

1) General information

Broad, general information has been found useful for predicting job success in some kinds of work. This is tested in a variety of ways, from vocabulary lists to questions about current events. Basic background in some field of work, such as sociology or economics, may be sampled in a group of questions. Often these are principles which have become familiar to most persons through exposure rather than through formal training. It is difficult to advise you how to study for these questions; being alert to the world around you is our best suggestion.

2) Verbal ability

An example of an ability needed in many positions is verbal or language ability. Verbal ability is, in brief, the ability to use and understand words. Vocabulary and grammar tests are typical measures of this ability. Reading comprehension or paragraph interpretation questions are common in many kinds of civil service tests. You are given a paragraph of written material and asked to find its central meaning.

3) Numerical ability

Number skills can be tested by the familiar arithmetic problem, by checking paired lists of numbers to see which are alike and which are different, or by interpreting charts and graphs. In the latter test, a graph may be printed in the test booklet which you are asked to use as the basis for answering questions.

4) Observation

A popular test for law-enforcement positions is the observation test. A picture is shown to you for several minutes, then taken away. Questions about the picture test your ability to observe both details and larger elements.

5) Following directions

In many positions in the public service, the employee must be able to carry out written instructions dependably and accurately. You may be given a chart with several columns, each column listing a variety of information. The questions require you to carry out directions involving the information given in the chart.

6) Skills and aptitudes

Performance tests effectively measure some manual skills and aptitudes. When the skill is one in which you are trained, such as typing or shorthand, you can practice. These tests are often very much like those given in business school or high school courses. For many of the other skills and aptitudes, however, no short-time preparation can be made. Skills and abilities natural to you or that you have developed throughout your lifetime are being tested.

Many of the general questions just described provide all the data needed to answer the questions and ask you to use your reasoning ability to find the answers. Your best preparation for these tests, as well as for tests of facts and ideas, is to be at your physical and mental best. You, no doubt, have your own methods of getting into an exam-taking mood and keeping "in shape." The next section lists some ideas on this subject.

IV. KINDS OF QUESTIONS

Only rarely is the "essay" question, which you answer in narrative form, used in civil service tests. Civil service tests are usually of the short-answer type. Full instructions for answering these questions will be given to you at the examination. But in case this is your first experience with short-answer questions and separate answer sheets, here is what you need to know:

1) Multiple-choice Questions

Most popular of the short-answer questions is the "multiple choice" or "best answer" question. It can be used, for example, to test for factual knowledge, ability to solve problems or judgment in meeting situations found at work.

A multiple-choice question is normally one of three types—
- It can begin with an incomplete statement followed by several possible endings. You are to find the one ending which *best* completes the statement, although some of the others may not be entirely wrong.
- It can also be a complete statement in the form of a question which is answered by choosing one of the statements listed.

- It can be in the form of a problem – again you select the best answer.

Here is an example of a multiple-choice question with a discussion which should give you some clues as to the method for choosing the right answer:

When an employee has a complaint about his assignment, the action which will *best* help him overcome his difficulty is to
- A. discuss his difficulty with his coworkers
- B. take the problem to the head of the organization
- C. take the problem to the person who gave him the assignment
- D. say nothing to anyone about his complaint

In answering this question, you should study each of the choices to find which is best. Consider choice "A" – Certainly an employee may discuss his complaint with fellow employees, but no change or improvement can result, and the complaint remains unresolved. Choice "B" is a poor choice since the head of the organization probably does not know what assignment you have been given, and taking your problem to him is known as "going over the head" of the supervisor. The supervisor, or person who made the assignment, is the person who can clarify it or correct any injustice. Choice "C" is, therefore, correct. To say nothing, as in choice "D," is unwise. Supervisors have and interest in knowing the problems employees are facing, and the employee is seeking a solution to his problem.

2) True/False Questions

The "true/false" or "right/wrong" form of question is sometimes used. Here a complete statement is given. Your job is to decide whether the statement is right or wrong.

SAMPLE: A roaming cell-phone call to a nearby city costs less than a non-roaming call to a distant city.

This statement is wrong, or false, since roaming calls are more expensive.

This is not a complete list of all possible question forms, although most of the others are variations of these common types. You will always get complete directions for answering questions. Be sure you understand *how* to mark your answers – ask questions until you do.

V. RECORDING YOUR ANSWERS

Computer terminals are used more and more today for many different kinds of exams.
For an examination with very few applicants, you may be told to record your answers in the test booklet itself. Separate answer sheets are much more common. If this separate answer sheet is to be scored by machine – and this is often the case – it is highly important that you mark your answers correctly in order to get credit.

An electronic scoring machine is often used in civil service offices because of the speed with which papers can be scored. Machine-scored answer sheets must be marked with a pencil, which will be given to you. This pencil has a high graphite content which responds to the electronic scoring machine. As a matter of fact, stray dots may register as answers, so do not let your pencil rest on the answer sheet while you are pondering the correct answer. Also, if your pencil lead breaks or is otherwise defective, ask for another.

Since the answer sheet will be dropped in a slot in the scoring machine, be careful not to bend the corners or get the paper crumpled.

The answer sheet normally has five vertical columns of numbers, with 30 numbers to a column. These numbers correspond to the question numbers in your test booklet. After each number, going across the page are four or five pairs of dotted lines. These short dotted lines have small letters or numbers above them. The first two pairs may also have a "T" or "F" above the letters. This indicates that the first two pairs only are to be used if the questions are of the true-false type. If the questions are multiple choice, disregard the "T" and "F" and pay attention only to the small letters or numbers.

Answer your questions in the manner of the sample that follows:

32. The largest city in the United States is
    A. Washington, D.C.
    B. New York City
    C. Chicago
    D. Detroit
    E. San Francisco

1) Choose the answer you think is best. (New York City is the largest, so "B" is correct.)
2) Find the row of dotted lines numbered the same as the question you are answering. (Find row number 32)
3) Find the pair of dotted lines corresponding to the answer. (Find the pair of lines under the mark "B.")
4) Make a solid black mark between the dotted lines.

VI. BEFORE THE TEST

Common sense will help you find procedures to follow to get ready for an examination. Too many of us, however, overlook these sensible measures. Indeed, nervousness and fatigue have been found to be the most serious reasons why applicants fail to do their best on civil service tests. Here is a list of reminders:

- Begin your preparation early – Don't wait until the last minute to go scurrying around for books and materials or to find out what the position is all about.
- Prepare continuously – An hour a night for a week is better than an all-night cram session. This has been definitely established. What is more, a night a week for a month will return better dividends than crowding your study into a shorter period of time.
- Locate the place of the exam – You have been sent a notice telling you when and where to report for the examination. If the location is in a different town or otherwise unfamiliar to you, it would be well to inquire the best route and learn something about the building.
- Relax the night before the test – Allow your mind to rest. Do not study at all that night. Plan some mild recreation or diversion; then go to bed early and get a good night's sleep.
- Get up early enough to make a leisurely trip to the place for the test – This way unforeseen events, traffic snarls, unfamiliar buildings, etc. will not upset you.
- Dress comfortably – A written test is not a fashion show. You will be known by number and not by name, so wear something comfortable.

- Leave excess paraphernalia at home – Shopping bags and odd bundles will get in your way. You need bring only the items mentioned in the official notice you received; usually everything you need is provided. Do not bring reference books to the exam. They will only confuse those last minutes and be taken away from you when in the test room.
- Arrive somewhat ahead of time – If because of transportation schedules you must get there very early, bring a newspaper or magazine to take your mind off yourself while waiting.
- Locate the examination room – When you have found the proper room, you will be directed to the seat or part of the room where you will sit. Sometimes you are given a sheet of instructions to read while you are waiting. Do not fill out any forms until you are told to do so; just read them and be prepared.
- Relax and prepare to listen to the instructions
- If you have any physical problem that may keep you from doing your best, be sure to tell the test administrator. If you are sick or in poor health, you really cannot do your best on the exam. You can come back and take the test some other time.

VII. AT THE TEST

The day of the test is here and you have the test booklet in your hand. The temptation to get going is very strong. Caution! There is more to success than knowing the right answers. You must know how to identify your papers and understand variations in the type of short-answer question used in this particular examination. Follow these suggestions for maximum results from your efforts:

1) Cooperate with the monitor

The test administrator has a duty to create a situation in which you can be as much at ease as possible. He will give instructions, tell you when to begin, check to see that you are marking your answer sheet correctly, and so on. He is not there to guard you, although he will see that your competitors do not take unfair advantage. He wants to help you do your best.

2) Listen to all instructions

Don't jump the gun! Wait until you understand all directions. In most civil service tests you get more time than you need to answer the questions. So don't be in a hurry. Read each word of instructions until you clearly understand the meaning. Study the examples, listen to all announcements and follow directions. Ask questions if you do not understand what to do.

3) Identify your papers

Civil service exams are usually identified by number only. You will be assigned a number; you must not put your name on your test papers. Be sure to copy your number correctly. Since more than one exam may be given, copy your exact examination title.

4) Plan your time

Unless you are told that a test is a "speed" or "rate of work" test, speed itself is usually not important. Time enough to answer all the questions will be provided, but this does not mean that you have all day. An overall time limit has been set. Divide the total time (in minutes) by the number of questions to determine the approximate time you have for each question.

5) Do not linger over difficult questions

If you come across a difficult question, mark it with a paper clip (useful to have along) and come back to it when you have been through the booklet. One caution if you do this – be sure to skip a number on your answer sheet as well. Check often to be sure that you have not lost your place and that you are marking in the row numbered the same as the question you are answering.

6) Read the questions

Be sure you know what the question asks! Many capable people are unsuccessful because they failed to *read* the questions correctly.

7) Answer all questions

Unless you have been instructed that a penalty will be deducted for incorrect answers, it is better to guess than to omit a question.

8) Speed tests

It is often better NOT to guess on speed tests. It has been found that on timed tests people are tempted to spend the last few seconds before time is called in marking answers at random – without even reading them – in the hope of picking up a few extra points. To discourage this practice, the instructions may warn you that your score will be "corrected" for guessing. That is, a penalty will be applied. The incorrect answers will be deducted from the correct ones, or some other penalty formula will be used.

9) Review your answers

If you finish before time is called, go back to the questions you guessed or omitted to give them further thought. Review other answers if you have time.

10) Return your test materials

If you are ready to leave before others have finished or time is called, take ALL your materials to the monitor and leave quietly. Never take any test material with you. The monitor can discover whose papers are not complete, and taking a test booklet may be grounds for disqualification.

VIII. EXAMINATION TECHNIQUES

1) Read the general instructions carefully. These are usually printed on the first page of the exam booklet. As a rule, these instructions refer to the timing of the examination; the fact that you should not start work until the signal and must stop work at a signal, etc. If there are any *special* instructions, such as a choice of questions to be answered, make sure that you note this instruction carefully.

2) When you are ready to start work on the examination, that is as soon as the signal has been given, read the instructions to each question booklet, underline any key words or phrases, such as *least, best, outline, describe* and the like. In this way you will tend to answer as requested rather than discover on reviewing your paper that you *listed without describing*, that you selected the *worst* choice rather than the *best* choice, etc.

3) If the examination is of the objective or multiple-choice type – that is, each question will also give a series of possible answers: A, B, C or D, and you are called upon to select the best answer and write the letter next to that answer on your answer paper – it is advisable to start answering each question in turn. There may be anywhere from 50 to 100 such questions in the three or four hours allotted and you can see how much time would be taken if you read through all the questions before beginning to answer any. Furthermore, if you come across a question or group of questions which you know would be difficult to answer, it would undoubtedly affect your handling of all the other questions.

4) If the examination is of the essay type and contains but a few questions, it is a moot point as to whether you should read all the questions before starting to answer any one. Of course, if you are given a choice – say five out of seven and the like – then it is essential to read all the questions so you can eliminate the two that are most difficult. If, however, you are asked to answer all the questions, there may be danger in trying to answer the easiest one first because you may find that you will spend too much time on it. The best technique is to answer the first question, then proceed to the second, etc.

5) Time your answers. Before the exam begins, write down the time it started, then add the time allowed for the examination and write down the time it must be completed, then divide the time available somewhat as follows:
   - If 3-1/2 hours are allowed, that would be 210 minutes. If you have 80 objective-type questions, that would be an average of 2-1/2 minutes per question. Allow yourself no more than 2 minutes per question, or a total of 160 minutes, which will permit about 50 minutes to review.
   - If for the time allotment of 210 minutes there are 7 essay questions to answer, that would average about 30 minutes a question. Give yourself only 25 minutes per question so that you have about 35 minutes to review.

6) The most important instruction is to *read each question* and make sure you know what is wanted. The second most important instruction is to *time yourself properly* so that you answer every question. The third most important instruction is to *answer every question*. Guess if you have to but include something for each question. Remember that you will receive no credit for a blank and will probably receive some credit if you write something in answer to an essay question. If you guess a letter – say "B" for a multiple-choice question – you may have guessed right. If you leave a blank as an answer to a multiple-choice question, the examiners may respect your feelings but it will not add a point to your score. Some exams may penalize you for wrong answers, so in such cases *only*, you may not want to guess unless you have some basis for your answer.

7) Suggestions
   a. Objective-type questions
      1. Examine the question booklet for proper sequence of pages and questions
      2. Read all instructions carefully
      3. Skip any question which seems too difficult; return to it after all other questions have been answered
      4. Apportion your time properly; do not spend too much time on any single question or group of questions

5. Note and underline key words – *all, most, fewest, least, best, worst, same, opposite,* etc.
6. Pay particular attention to negatives
7. Note unusual option, e.g., unduly long, short, complex, different or similar in content to the body of the question
8. Observe the use of "hedging" words – *probably, may, most likely,* etc.
9. Make sure that your answer is put next to the same number as the question
10. Do not second-guess unless you have good reason to believe the second answer is definitely more correct
11. Cross out original answer if you decide another answer is more accurate; do not erase until you are ready to hand your paper in
12. Answer all questions; guess unless instructed otherwise
13. Leave time for review

b. Essay questions
1. Read each question carefully
2. Determine exactly what is wanted. Underline key words or phrases.
3. Decide on outline or paragraph answer
4. Include many different points and elements unless asked to develop any one or two points or elements
5. Show impartiality by giving pros and cons unless directed to select one side only
6. Make and write down any assumptions you find necessary to answer the questions
7. Watch your English, grammar, punctuation and choice of words
8. Time your answers; don't crowd material

8) Answering the essay question

Most essay questions can be answered by framing the specific response around several key words or ideas. Here are a few such key words or ideas:

M's: manpower, materials, methods, money, management
P's: purpose, program, policy, plan, procedure, practice, problems, pitfalls, personnel, public relations

a. Six basic steps in handling problems:
1. Preliminary plan and background development
2. Collect information, data and facts
3. Analyze and interpret information, data and facts
4. Analyze and develop solutions as well as make recommendations
5. Prepare report and sell recommendations
6. Install recommendations and follow up effectiveness

b. Pitfalls to avoid
1. *Taking things for granted* – A statement of the situation does not necessarily imply that each of the elements is necessarily true; for example, a complaint may be invalid and biased so that all that can be taken for granted is that a complaint has been registered

2. *Considering only one side of a situation* – Wherever possible, indicate several alternatives and then point out the reasons you selected the best one
3. *Failing to indicate follow up* – Whenever your answer indicates action on your part, make certain that you will take proper follow-up action to see how successful your recommendations, procedures or actions turn out to be
4. *Taking too long in answering any single question* – Remember to time your answers properly

IX. AFTER THE TEST

Scoring procedures differ in detail among civil service jurisdictions although the general principles are the same. Whether the papers are hand-scored or graded by machine we have described, they are nearly always graded by number. That is, the person who marks the paper knows only the number – never the name – of the applicant. Not until all the papers have been graded will they be matched with names. If other tests, such as training and experience or oral interview ratings have been given, scores will be combined. Different parts of the examination usually have different weights. For example, the written test might count 60 percent of the final grade, and a rating of training and experience 40 percent. In many jurisdictions, veterans will have a certain number of points added to their grades.

After the final grade has been determined, the names are placed in grade order and an eligible list is established. There are various methods for resolving ties between those who get the same final grade – probably the most common is to place first the name of the person whose application was received first. Job offers are made from the eligible list in the order the names appear on it. You will be notified of your grade and your rank as soon as all these computations have been made. This will be done as rapidly as possible.

People who are found to meet the requirements in the announcement are called "eligibles." Their names are put on a list of eligible candidates. An eligible's chances of getting a job depend on how high he stands on this list and how fast agencies are filling jobs from the list.

When a job is to be filled from a list of eligibles, the agency asks for the names of people on the list of eligibles for that job. When the civil service commission receives this request, it sends to the agency the names of the three people highest on this list. Or, if the job to be filled has specialized requirements, the office sends the agency the names of the top three persons who meet these requirements from the general list.

The appointing officer makes a choice from among the three people whose names were sent to him. If the selected person accepts the appointment, the names of the others are put back on the list to be considered for future openings.

That is the rule in hiring from all kinds of eligible lists, whether they are for typist, carpenter, chemist, or something else. For every vacancy, the appointing officer has his choice of any one of the top three eligibles on the list. This explains why the person whose name is on top of the list sometimes does not get an appointment when some of the persons lower on the list do. If the appointing officer chooses the second or third eligible, the No. 1 eligible does not get a job at once, but stays on the list until he is appointed or the list is terminated.

X. HOW TO PASS THE INTERVIEW TEST

The examination for which you applied requires an oral interview test. You have already taken the written test and you are now being called for the interview test – the final part of the formal examination.

You may think that it is not possible to prepare for an interview test and that there are no procedures to follow during an interview. Our purpose is to point out some things you can do in advance that will help you and some good rules to follow and pitfalls to avoid while you are being interviewed.

What is an interview supposed to test?

The written examination is designed to test the technical knowledge and competence of the candidate; the oral is designed to evaluate intangible qualities, not readily measured otherwise, and to establish a list showing the relative fitness of each candidate – as measured against his competitors – for the position sought. Scoring is not on the basis of "right" and "wrong," but on a sliding scale of values ranging from "not passable" to "outstanding." As a matter of fact, it is possible to achieve a relatively low score without a single "incorrect" answer because of evident weakness in the qualities being measured.

Occasionally, an examination may consist entirely of an oral test – either an individual or a group oral. In such cases, information is sought concerning the technical knowledges and abilities of the candidate, since there has been no written examination for this purpose. More commonly, however, an oral test is used to supplement a written examination.

Who conducts interviews?

The composition of oral boards varies among different jurisdictions. In nearly all, a representative of the personnel department serves as chairman. One of the members of the board may be a representative of the department in which the candidate would work. In some cases, "outside experts" are used, and, frequently, a businessman or some other representative of the general public is asked to serve. Labor and management or other special groups may be represented. The aim is to secure the services of experts in the appropriate field.

However the board is composed, it is a good idea (and not at all improper or unethical) to ascertain in advance of the interview who the members are and what groups they represent. When you are introduced to them, you will have some idea of their backgrounds and interests, and at least you will not stutter and stammer over their names.

What should be done before the interview?

While knowledge about the board members is useful and takes some of the surprise element out of the interview, there is other preparation which is more substantive. It *is* possible to prepare for an oral interview – in several ways:

1) Keep a copy of your application and review it carefully before the interview

This may be the only document before the oral board, and the starting point of the interview. Know what education and experience you have listed there, and the sequence and dates of all of it. Sometimes the board will ask you to review the highlights of your experience for them; you should not have to hem and haw doing it.

2) Study the class specification and the examination announcement

Usually, the oral board has one or both of these to guide them. The qualities, characteristics or knowledges required by the position sought are stated in these documents. They offer valuable clues as to the nature of the oral interview. For example, if the job involves supervisory responsibilities, the announcement will usually indicate that knowledge of modern supervisory methods and the qualifications of the candidate as a supervisor will be tested. If so, you can expect such questions, frequently in the form of a hypothetical situation which you are expected to solve. NEVER go into an oral without knowledge of the duties and responsibilities of the job you seek.

3) Think through each qualification required

Try to visualize the kind of questions you would ask if you were a board member. How well could you answer them? Try especially to appraise your own knowledge and background in each area, *measured against the job sought*, and identify any areas in which you are weak. Be critical and realistic – do not flatter yourself.

4) Do some general reading in areas in which you feel you may be weak

For example, if the job involves supervision and your past experience has NOT, some general reading in supervisory methods and practices, particularly in the field of human relations, might be useful. Do NOT study agency procedures or detailed manuals. The oral board will be testing your understanding and capacity, not your memory.

5) Get a good night's sleep and watch your general health and mental attitude

You will want a clear head at the interview. Take care of a cold or any other minor ailment, and of course, no hangovers.

What should be done on the day of the interview?

Now comes the day of the interview itself. Give yourself plenty of time to get there. Plan to arrive somewhat ahead of the scheduled time, particularly if your appointment is in the fore part of the day. If a previous candidate fails to appear, the board might be ready for you a bit early. By early afternoon an oral board is almost invariably behind schedule if there are many candidates, and you may have to wait. Take along a book or magazine to read, or your application to review, but leave any extraneous material in the waiting room when you go in for your interview. In any event, relax and compose yourself.

The matter of dress is important. The board is forming impressions about you – from your experience, your manners, your attitude, and your appearance. Give your personal appearance careful attention. Dress your best, but not your flashiest. Choose conservative, appropriate clothing, and be sure it is immaculate. This is a business interview, and your appearance should indicate that you regard it as such. Besides, being well groomed and properly dressed will help boost your confidence.

Sooner or later, someone will call your name and escort you into the interview room. *This is it.* From here on you are on your own. It is too late for any more preparation. But remember, you asked for this opportunity to prove your fitness, and you are here because your request was granted.

What happens when you go in?

The usual sequence of events will be as follows: The clerk (who is often the board stenographer) will introduce you to the chairman of the oral board, who will introduce you to the other members of the board. Acknowledge the introductions before you sit down. Do not be surprised if you find a microphone facing you or a stenotypist sitting by. Oral interviews are usually recorded in the event of an appeal or other review.

Usually the chairman of the board will open the interview by reviewing the highlights of your education and work experience from your application – primarily for the benefit of the other members of the board, as well as to get the material into the record. Do not interrupt or comment unless there is an error or significant misinterpretation; if that is the case, do not hesitate. But do not quibble about insignificant matters. Also, he will usually ask you some question about your education, experience or your present job – partly to get you to start talking and to establish the interviewing "rapport." He may start the actual questioning, or turn it over to one of the other members. Frequently, each member undertakes the questioning on a particular area, one in which he is perhaps most competent, so you can expect each member to participate in the examination. Because time is limited, you may also expect some rather abrupt switches in the direction the questioning takes, so do not be upset by it. Normally, a board member will not pursue a single line of questioning unless he discovers a particular strength or weakness.

After each member has participated, the chairman will usually ask whether any member has any further questions, then will ask you if you have anything you wish to add. Unless you are expecting this question, it may floor you. Worse, it may start you off on an extended, extemporaneous speech. The board is not usually seeking more information. The question is principally to offer you a last opportunity to present further qualifications or to indicate that you have nothing to add. So, if you feel that a significant qualification or characteristic has been overlooked, it is proper to point it out in a sentence or so. Do not compliment the board on the thoroughness of their examination – they have been sketchy, and you know it. If you wish, merely say, "No thank you, I have nothing further to add." This is a point where you can "talk yourself out" of a good impression or fail to present an important bit of information. Remember, *you close the interview yourself.*

The chairman will then say, "That is all, Mr. _____, thank you." Do not be startled; the interview is over, and quicker than you think. Thank him, gather your belongings and take your leave. Save your sigh of relief for the other side of the door.

How to put your best foot forward
Throughout this entire process, you may feel that the board individually and collectively is trying to pierce your defenses, seek out your hidden weaknesses and embarrass and confuse you. Actually, this is not true. They are obliged to make an appraisal of your qualifications for the job you are seeking, and they want to see you in your best light. Remember, they must interview all candidates and a non-cooperative candidate may become a failure in spite of their best efforts to bring out his qualifications. Here are 15 suggestions that will help you:

1) Be natural – Keep your attitude confident, not cocky
If you are not confident that you can do the job, do not expect the board to be. Do not apologize for your weaknesses, try to bring out your strong points. The board is interested in a positive, not negative, presentation. Cockiness will antagonize any board member and make him wonder if you are covering up a weakness by a false show of strength.

2) Get comfortable, but don't lounge or sprawl
Sit erectly but not stiffly. A careless posture may lead the board to conclude that you are careless in other things, or at least that you are not impressed by the importance of the occasion. Either conclusion is natural, even if incorrect. Do not fuss with your clothing, a pencil or an ashtray. Your hands may occasionally be useful to emphasize a point; do not let them become a point of distraction.

3) Do not wisecrack or make small talk
This is a serious situation, and your attitude should show that you consider it as such. Further, the time of the board is limited – they do not want to waste it, and neither should you.

4) Do not exaggerate your experience or abilities

In the first place, from information in the application or other interviews and sources, the board may know more about you than you think. Secondly, you probably will not get away with it. An experienced board is rather adept at spotting such a situation, so do not take the chance.

5) If you know a board member, do not make a point of it, yet do not hide it

Certainly you are not fooling him, and probably not the other members of the board. Do not try to take advantage of your acquaintanceship – it will probably do you little good.

6) Do not dominate the interview

Let the board do that. They will give you the clues – do not assume that you have to do all the talking. Realize that the board has a number of questions to ask you, and do not try to take up all the interview time by showing off your extensive knowledge of the answer to the first one.

7) Be attentive

You only have 20 minutes or so, and you should keep your attention at its sharpest throughout. When a member is addressing a problem or question to you, give him your undivided attention. Address your reply principally to him, but do not exclude the other board members.

8) Do not interrupt

A board member may be stating a problem for you to analyze. He will ask you a question when the time comes. Let him state the problem, and wait for the question.

9) Make sure you understand the question

Do not try to answer until you are sure what the question is. If it is not clear, restate it in your own words or ask the board member to clarify it for you. However, do not haggle about minor elements.

10) Reply promptly but not hastily

A common entry on oral board rating sheets is "candidate responded readily," or "candidate hesitated in replies." Respond as promptly and quickly as you can, but do not jump to a hasty, ill-considered answer.

11) Do not be peremptory in your answers

A brief answer is proper – but do not fire your answer back. That is a losing game from your point of view. The board member can probably ask questions much faster than you can answer them.

12) Do not try to create the answer you think the board member wants

He is interested in what kind of mind you have and how it works – not in playing games. Furthermore, he can usually spot this practice and will actually grade you down on it.

13) Do not switch sides in your reply merely to agree with a board member

Frequently, a member will take a contrary position merely to draw you out and to see if you are willing and able to defend your point of view. Do not start a debate, yet do not surrender a good position. If a position is worth taking, it is worth defending.

14) Do not be afraid to admit an error in judgment if you are shown to be wrong

The board knows that you are forced to reply without any opportunity for careful consideration. Your answer may be demonstrably wrong. If so, admit it and get on with the interview.

15) Do not dwell at length on your present job

The opening question may relate to your present assignment. Answer the question but do not go into an extended discussion. You are being examined for a *new* job, not your present one. As a matter of fact, try to phrase ALL your answers in terms of the job for which you are being examined.

Basis of Rating

Probably you will forget most of these "do's" and "don'ts" when you walk into the oral interview room. Even remembering them all will not ensure you a passing grade. Perhaps you did not have the qualifications in the first place. But remembering them will help you to put your best foot forward, without treading on the toes of the board members.

Rumor and popular opinion to the contrary notwithstanding, an oral board wants you to make the best appearance possible. They know you are under pressure – but they also want to see how you respond to it as a guide to what your reaction would be under the pressures of the job you seek. They will be influenced by the degree of poise you display, the personal traits you show and the manner in which you respond.

ABOUT THIS BOOK

This book contains tests divided into Examination Sections. Go through each test, answering every question in the margin. We have also attached a sample answer sheet at the back of the book that can be removed and used. At the end of each test look at the answer key and check your answers. On the ones you got wrong, look at the right answer choice and learn. Do not fill in the answers first. Do not memorize the questions and answers, but understand the answer and principles involved. On your test, the questions will likely be different from the samples. Questions are changed and new ones added. If you understand these past questions you should have success with any changes that arise. Tests may consist of several types of questions. We have additional books on each subject should more study be advisable or necessary for you. Finally, the more you study, the better prepared you will be. This book is intended to be the last thing you study before you walk into the examination room. Prior study of relevant texts is also recommended. NLC publishes some of these in our Fundamental Series. Knowledge and good sense are important factors in passing your exam. Good luck also helps. So now study this Passbook, absorb the material contained within and take that knowledge into the examination. Then do your best to pass that exam.

EXAMINATION SECTION

EXAMINATION SECTION
TEST 1

DIRECTIONS: Each question or incomplete statement is followed by several suggested answers or completions. Select the one that BEST answers the question or completes the statement. *PRINT THE LETTER OF THE CORRECT ANSWER IN THE SPACE AT THE RIGHT.*

Questions 1-8.

DIRECTIONS: Each of Questions 1 through 8 consists of a statement which contains a word (one of those underlined) that is either incorrectly used because it is not in keeping with the meaning the quotation is evidently intended to convey or is misspelled. There is only one INCORRECT word in each quotation. Of the four underlined words, determine if the first one should be replaced by the word lettered A, the second replaced by the word lettered B, the third replaced by the word lettered C, or the fourth replaced by the word lettered D. Print the letter of the replacement word you have selected in the space at the right.

1. Whether one depends on fluorescent or artificial light or both, adequate standards should be maintained by means of systematic tests.
   A. natural   B. safeguards   C. established   D. routine

       1.____

2. An officer has to be prepared to assume his knowledge as a social scientist in the community.
   A. forced   B. role   C. philosopher   D. street

       2.____

3. It is practically impossible to indicate whether a sentence is too long simply by measuring its length.
   A. almost   B. tell   C. very   D. guessing

       3.____

4. Strong leaders are required to organize a community for delinquency prevention and for dissemination of organized crime and drug addiction.
   A. tactics   B. important   C. control   D. meetings

       4.____

5. The demonstrators, who were taken to the Criminal Courts building in Manhattan (because it was large enough to accommodate them), contended that the arrests were unwarrented.
   A. exhibitors   B. legions   C. adjudicate   D. unwarranted

       5.____

6. The were guaranteed a calm atmosphere, free from harassment, which would be conducive to quiet consideration of the indictments.
   A. guaranted   B. atmospher   C. harassment   D. inditements

       6.____

7. The alleged killer was occasionally permitted to excercise in the corridor.
   A. alledged   B. ocasionally   C. permited   D. exercise

       7.____

8. Defense <u>counsel</u> stated, in <u>affect</u>, that <u>their</u> conduct was <u>permissable</u> under the First Amendment.
   A. council   B. effect   C. there   D. permissable

8.____

Questions 9-12.

DIRECTIONS: Each of the two sentences in Questions 9 through 12 may be correct or may contain errors in punctuation, capitalization, or grammar. If there is an error only in sentence I, mark your answer A. If there is an error in both sentence I and sentence II, mark your answer C. If both sentence I and sentence II are correct, mark your answer D.

9. I. It is very annoying to have a pencil sharpener, which is not in working order.
   II. Officer Blake checked the door of Joe's Restaurant and found that the lock has been jammed.

9.____

10. I. When you are studying a good textbook is important.
   II. He said he would divide the money equally between you and me.

10.____

11. I. Since he went on the city council a year ago, one of his primary concerns has been safety in the streets.
   II. After waiting in the doorway for about 15 minutes, a black sedan appeared.

11.____

12. I. The question is, "What is the difference between a lawful and an unlawful demonstration?"
   II. The captain assigned two detectives, John and I, to the investigation.

12.____

Questions 13-14.

DIRECTIONS: In each of Questions 13 and 14, the four sentences are from a paragraph in a report. They are not in the right order. Which of the following arrangement is the BEST one?

13. I. Most organizations favor one of the types but always include the others to a lesser degree.
   II. However, we can detect a definite trend toward greater use of symbolic control.
   III. We suggest that our local police agencies are today primarily utilizing material control.
   IV. Control can be classified into three types: physical, material, and symbolic.
The CORRECT answer is:
   A. IV, II III, I   B. II, I, IV, III   C. III, IV, II, I   D. IV, I, III, II

13.____

14. I They can and do take advantage of ancient political and geographical boundaries, which often give them sanctuary from effective policy activity.
   II. This country is essentially a country of small police forces, each operating independently within the limits of its jurisdiction.

14.____

III. The boundaries that define and limit police operations do not hinder the movement of criminals, of course.
IV. The machinery of law enforcement in America is fragmented, complicated, and frequently overlapping.

The CORRECT answer is
A. III, I, II, IV   B. II, IV, I, III   C. IV, II, III, I   D. IV, III, II, I

15. Generally, the frequency with which reports are to be submitted or the length of the interval which they cover should depend MAINLY on the
    A. amount of time needed to prepare the reports
    B. degree of comprehensiveness required in the reports
    C. availability of the data to be included in the reports
    D. extent of the variations in the data with the passage of time

16. Suppose you have to write a report on a serious infraction of rules by one of the police administrative aides you supervise. The circumstances in which the infraction occurred are quite complicated.
    The BEST way to organize this report would be to
    A. give all points equal emphasis throughout the report
    B. include more than one point in a paragraph only if necessary to equalize the size of paragraphs
    C. place the least important points before the most important points
    D. present each significant point in a separate paragraph

17. Suppose that police expenses in the city in a certain year amounted to 7.5% of total expenses.
    In indicating this percentage on a *pie* or circular chart, which is 360, the size of the angle between the two radiuses would be MOST NEARLY
    A. 3.7   B. 7.5   C. 27   D. 54

18. Suppose that in police precinct A, where there are 4,180 children, 627 children entered a contest sponsored by the Police Community Relations Bureau. In precinct B, where there were 7,840 children, 1,960 children entered the contest.
    The total percentage of all children in both precincts who entered the contest amounted to MOST NEARLY
    A. 19.5%   B. 20%   C. 21.5%   D. 22.5%

19. If Circle A represents Police Administrative Aides (PAA's) who scored above 85 on a PAA test and Circle B represents PAA's who scored above 85 on a Senior PAA test, then the diagram at the right means that
    A. no PAA who scored above 85 on a PAA test scored above 85 on the Senior PAA test
    B. the majority of PAA's who scored above 85 on a PAA test scored above 85 on the Senior PAA test
    C. there were some PAA's who did not take the Senior PAA test
    D. some PAA's who scored above 85 on a PAA test scored above 85 on the Senior PAA test

20. Suppose that in 1912 the city had a population of 550,000 and a police force of 200, and that in 2012 the city had a population of 8,000,000 and a police force of 32,000.
If the ratio of police to population in 2012 is compared with the same ratio in 1912, what is the resulting relationship of the 2012 ratio to the 1912 ratio?
A. 160:11   B. 160:1   C. 16:1   D. 11:1

20.____

Questions 21-24.

DIRECTIONS: Questions 21 through 24 are to be answered SOLELY on the basis of the information contained in the following passage.

Of those arrested in the city in 2019 for felonies or misdemeanors, only 32% were found guilty of any charge. Fifty-six percent of such arrestees were acquitted or had their cases dismissed, 11% failed to appear for trial, and 1% received other dispositions. Of those found guilty, only 7.4% received any sentences of over one year in jail. Only 50% of those found guilty were sentenced to any further time in jail. When considered with the low probability of arrests for most crimes, these figures make it clear that the crime control system in the city poses little threat to the average criminal. Delay compounds the problem. The average case took four appearances for disposition after arraignment. Twenty percent of all cases took eight or more appearances to reach a disposition. Forty-four percent of all cases took more than one year to disposition.

21. According to the above passage, crime statistics for 2019 indicate that
A. there is a low probability of arrests for all crimes in the city
B. the average criminal has much to fear from the law in the city
C. over 10% of arrestees in the city charged with felonies or misdemeanors did not show up for trial
D. criminals in the city are less likely to be caught than criminals in the rest f the country

21.____

22. The percentage of those arrested in 2019 who received sentences of over one year in jail amounted MOST NEARLY to
A. .237   B. 2.4   C. 23.7   D. 24.0

22.____

23. According to the above passage, the percentage of arrestees in 2019 who were found guilty was
A 20% of those arrested for misdemeanors
B. 11% of those arrested for felonies
C. 50% of those sentenced to further time in jail
D. 32% of those arrested for felonies or misdemeanors

23.____

24. According to the above passage, the number of appearances after arraignment and before disposition amounted to
A. an average of four
B. eight or more in 44% of the cases
C. over four for cases which took more than a year
D. between four and eight for most cases

24.____

Questions 25-27.

DIRECTIONS: Questions 25 through 27 are to be answered SOLELY on the basis of the information contained in the following passage.

The traditional characteristics of a police organization, which do not foster group-centered leadership, are being changed daily by progressive police administrators. These characteristics are authoritarian and result in a leader-centered style with all determination of policy and procedure made by the leader. In the group-centered style, policies and procedures are a matter for group discussion and decision. The supposedly modern view is that the group-centered style is the most conducive to improving organizational effectiveness. By contrast, the traditional view regards the group-centered style as an idealistic notion of psychologists. It is questionable, however, that the situation determines the appropriate leadership style. In some circumstances, it will be leader-centered; in others, group-centered. Nevertheless, police supervisors will see more situations calling for a leadership style that, while flexible, is primarily group-centered. Thus, the supervisor in a police department must have a capacity not just to issue orders but to engage in behavior involving organizational leadership which primarily emphasizes goals and work facilitation.

25. According to the above passage, there is reason to believe that with regard to the effectiveness of different types of leadership, the
    A. leader-centered type is better than the individual-centered type or the group-centered type
    B. leader-centered type is best in some situations and the group-centered type best in other situations
    C. group-centered type is better than the leader-centered type in all situations
    D. authoritarian type is least effective in democratic countries

26. According to the above passage, police administrators today are
    A. more likely than in the past to favor making decisions on the basis of discussions with subordinates
    B. likely in general to favor traditional patterns of leadership in their organizations
    C. more likely to be progressive than conservative
    D. practical and individualistic rather than idealistic in their approach to police problems

27. According to the above passage, the role of the police department is changing in such a way that its supervisors must
    A. give greater consideration to the needs of individual subordinates
    B. be more flexible in dealing with infractions of department rules
    C. provide leadership which stresses the goals of the department and helps the staff to reach them
    D. refrain from issuing orders and allow subordinates to decide how to carry out their assignments

Questions 28-31.

DIRECTIONS: Questions 28 through 31 are to be answered SOLELY on the basis of the information contained in the following passage.

Under the provisions of the Bank Protection Act of 1968, enacted July 8, 1968, each Federal banking supervisory agency, as of January 7, 1969, had to issue rules establishing minimum standards with which financial institutions under their control must comply with respect to the installation, maintenance, and operation of security devices and procedures, reasonable in cost, to discourage robberies, burglaries, and larcenies, and to assist in the identification and apprehension of persons who commit such acts. The rules set the time limits within which the affected banks and savings and loan associations must comply with the standards, and the rules require the submission of periodic reports on the steps taken. A violator of a rule under this Act is subject to a civil penalty not to exceed $100 for each day of the violation. The enforcement of these regulations rests with the responsible banking supervisory agencies.

28. The Bank Protection Act of 1968 was designed to
    A. provide Federal police protection for banks covered by the Act
    B. have organizations covered by the Act take precautions against criminals
    C. set up a system for reporting all bank robberies to the FBI
    D. insure institutions covered by the Act from financial loss due to robberies, burglaries, and larcenies

29. Under the provisions of the Bank Protection Act of 1968, each Federal banking supervisory agency was required to set up rules for financial institutions covered by the Act governing the
    A. hiring of personnel
    B. punishment of burglars
    C. taking of protective measures
    D. penalties for violations

30. Financial institutions covered by the Bank Protection Act of 1968 were required to
    A. file reports at regular intervals on what they had done to prevent theft
    B. identify and apprehend persons who commit robberies, burglaries, and larcenies
    C. draw up a code of ethics for their employees
    D. have fingerprints of their employees filed with the FBI

31. Under the provisions of the Bank Protection Act of 1968, a bank which is subject to the rules established under the Act and which violates a rule is liable to a penalty of NOT _____ than $100 for each _____.
    A. more; violation
    B. less; day of violation
    C. less; violation
    D. more; day of violation

Questions 32-36.

DIRECTIONS: Questions 32 through 36 are to be answered SOLELY on the basis of the information contained in the following passage.

A statement which is offered in an attempt to prove the truth of the matters therein stated, but which is not made by the author as a witness before the court at the particular trial in which it is so offered, is hearsay. This is so whether the statement consists of words (oral or written), of symbols used as a substitute for words, or of signs or other conduct offered as the equivalent of a statement. Subject to some well-established exceptions, hearsay is not generally acceptable as evidence, and it does not become competent evidence just because it is received by the court without objection. One basis for this rule is simply that a fact cannot be proved by showing that somebody stated it was a fact. Another basis for the rule is the fundamental principle that in a criminal prosecution the testimony of the witness shall be taken before the court, so that at the time he gives the testimony offered in evidence he will be sworn and subject to cross-examination, the scrutiny of the court, and confrontation by the accused.

32. Which of the following is hearsay? A(n)
    A. written statement by a person not present at the court hearing where the statement is submitted as proof of an occurrence
    B. oral statement in court by a witness of what he saw
    C. written statement of what he saw by a witness present in court
    D. re-enactment by a witness in court of what he saw

33. In a criminal case, a statement by a person not present in court is
    A. *acceptable* evidence if not objected to by the prosecutor
    B. *acceptable* evidence if not objected to by the defense lawyer
    C. *not acceptable* evidence except in certain well-settled circumstances
    D. *not acceptable* evidence under any circumstances

34. The rule on hearsay is founded on the belief that
    A. proving someone said an act occurred is not proof that the act did occur
    B. a person who has knowledge about a case should be willing to appear in court
    C. persons not present in court are likely to be unreliable witnesses
    D. permitting persons to testify without appearing in court will lead to a disrespect for law

35. One reason for the general rule that a witness in a criminal case must give his testimony in court is that
    A. a witness may be influenced by threats to make untrue statements
    B. the opposite side is then permitted to question him
    C. the court provides protection for a witness against unfair questioning
    D. the adversary system is designed to prevent a miscarriage of justice

36. Of the following, the MOST appropriate title for the above passage would be
    A. What is Hearsay
    B. Rights of Defendants
    C. Trial procedures
    D. Testimony of Witnesses

Questions 37-40.

DIRECTIONS: Questions 37 through 40 are to be answered SOLELY on the basis of the following graphs.

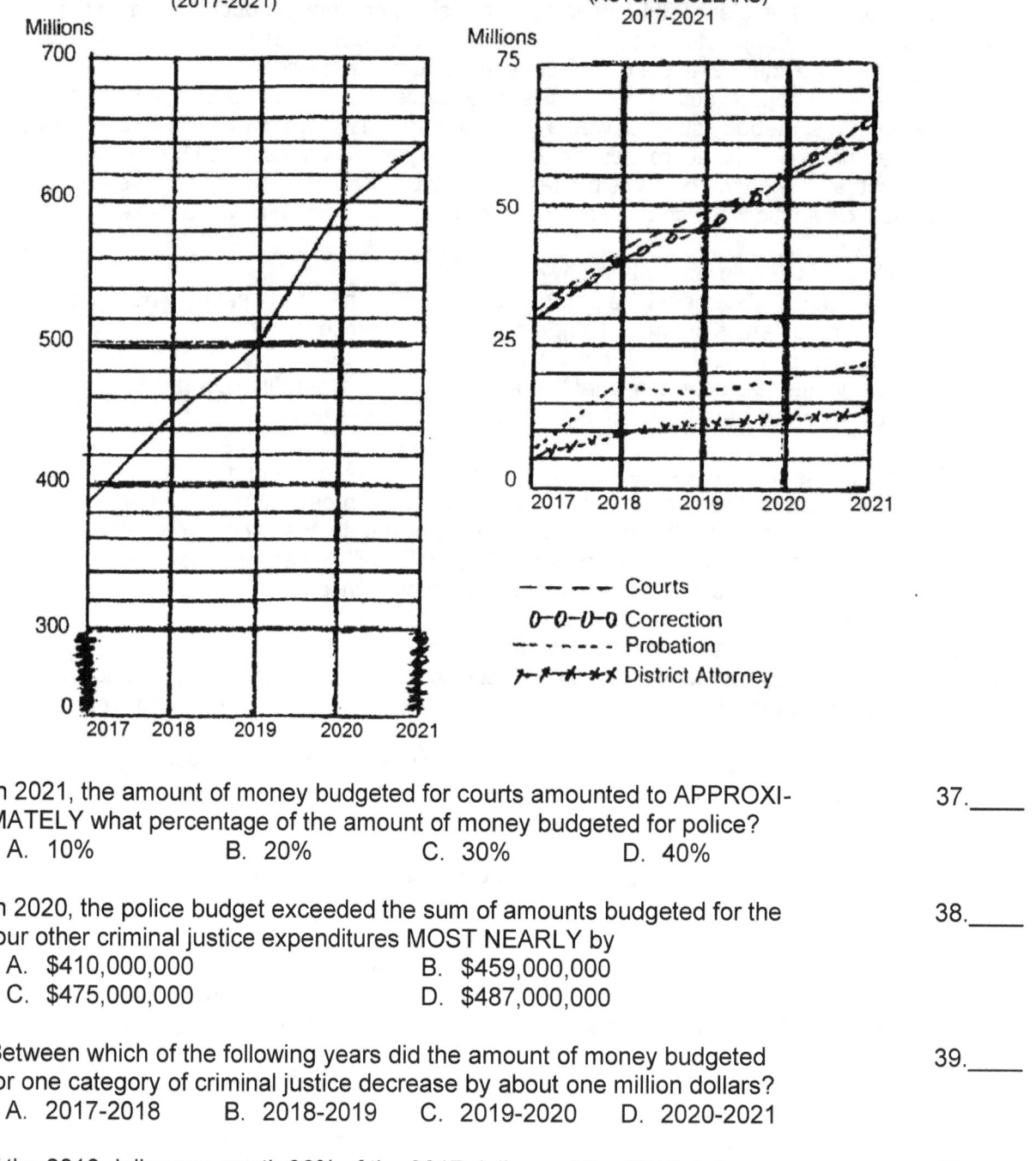

37. In 2021, the amount of money budgeted for courts amounted to APPROXIMATELY what percentage of the amount of money budgeted for police?
    A. 10%   B. 20%   C. 30%   D. 40%

38. In 2020, the police budget exceeded the sum of amounts budgeted for the four other criminal justice expenditures MOST NEARLY by
    A. $410,000,000
    B. $459,000,000
    C. $475,000,000
    D. $487,000,000

39. Between which of the following years did the amount of money budgeted for one category of criminal justice decrease by about one million dollars?
    A. 2017-2018   B. 2018-2019   C. 2019-2020   D. 2020-2021

40. If the 2018 dollar was worth 96% of the 2017 dollar and the 2019 dollar was worth 90% of the 2017 dollar, the increase in the budget for Correction from 2018 to 2019, in terms of the 2017 dollar, amounted to
    A. $2,100,000   B. $4,200,000   C. $4,320,000   D. $4,700,000

KEY (CORRECT ANSWERS)

1.	A	11.	C	21.	C	31.	D
2.	B	12.	B	22.	B	32.	A
3.	B	13.	D	23.	D	33.	C
4.	C	14.	C	24.	A	34.	A
5.	D	15.	D	25.	B	35.	B
6.	C	16.	D	26.	A	36.	A
7.	D	17.	C	27.	C	37.	A
8.	B	18.	C	28.	B	38.	B
9.	C	19.	D	29.	C	39.	B
10.	A	20.	D	30.	A	40.	A

EXAMINATION SECTION
TEST 1

DIRECTIONS: Each question or incomplete statement is followed by several suggested answers or completions. Select the one that BEST answers the question or completes the statement. *PRINT THE LETTER OF THE CORRECT ANSWER IN THE SPACE AT THE RIGHT.*

1. You answer a phone complaint from a person concerning an improper labeling practice in a shop in his neighborhood. Upon listening to the complaint, you get the impression that the person is exaggerating and may be too excited to view the matter clearly.
   Of the following, your BEST course would be to
   A. tell the man that you can understand his anger but think it is not a really serious problem
   B. suggest to the man that he file a complaint with the Department of Consumer Affairs
   C. tell the man to stay away from the shop and have his friends do the same
   D. take down the information that the man offers so that he will see that the Police Department is concerned

1.____

2. Suppose that late at night you receive a call on 911. The caller turns out to be an elderly man who is not able to get out much and who is calling you not because he needs help but because he wants to talk with someone.
   The BEST way to handle such a situation is to
   A. explain to him that the number is for emergencies and his call may prevent others from getting the help they need
   B. talk to him if not many calls are coming in but excuse yourself and cut him off if you are busy
   C. cut him off immediately when you find out he does not need help because this will be the most effective way of discouraging him
   D. suggest that he call train or bus information as the clerks there are often not busy at night

2.____

3. While you are on duty, you receive a call from a person whose name your recognize to be that of a person who calls frequently about matters of no importance. The caller requests your name and your supervisor's name so that she can report you for being impolite to her.
   You should
   A. ask her when and how you were impolite to her
   B. tell her that she should not call about such minor matters
   C. make a report about her complaint for your superior
   D. give her the information that she requests

3.____

4. Of the following, the MOST important reason for requiring each employ of the Police Department to be responsible for good public relations is that
   A. the Police Department has better morale when employees join in an effort to improve public relations
   B. the public judges the Department according to impressions received at every level in the Department
   C. most employees will not behave well toward the public unless required to do so
   D. employees who improve public relations will receive commendations from superiors

5. Assume that you are in the Bureau of Public Relations. You receive a telephone call from a citizen who asks if a study has been made of the advisability of combining the city's police and fire departments. Assume that you have no information on the subject.
   Of the following, your BEST course would be to
   A. tell the caller that undoubtedly the subject has been studied but that you do not have the information available
   B. suggest to the caller that he telephone the Fire Department's Community Relations section for further information
   C. explain to the caller that the functions of the two departments are distinct and that combining them would be inefficient
   D. take the caller's number in order to call back, and then find information or referrals to give him

6. Suppose that Police Department officials have discouraged representatives of the press from contacting police administrative aides (except aides in the Public Relations Bureau) for information.
   Of the following, the BEST reason for such a policy would be to
   A. assure proper control over information released to the press by the Department
   B. increase the value of official press releases of the Department
   C. make press representatives realize that the Department is not seeking publicity
   D. reduce the chance of crimes being committed in imitation of those reported in the press

7. People who phone the Police Department often use excited, emotional, and sometimes angry speech.
   The BEST policy for you to take when speaking to this type of caller is to
   A. tell the person directly that he must speak in a more civil way
   B. tell the caller to call back when he is in a better mood
   C. give the person time to settle down, by doing most of the talking yourself
   D. speak calmly yourself to help the caller to gradually become more relaxed

3 (#1)

8. On a particularly busy evening, the police administrative aide assigned to the telephones had answered a tremendous number of inquiries and complaints by irate citizens. His patience was exhausted when he received a call from a citizen who reported, *Officer, a bird just flew into my bedroom. What should I do?* In a release of tension, the aide responded, *Keep it for seven days; and if no one claims it, it is yours.*
    This response by the aide would usually be considered
    A. *advisable*, because the person should see how unusual his question was
    B. *advisable*, because he avoided offering police services that were unavailable
    C. *not advisable*, because such a remark might be regarded as insulting rather than humorous
    D. *not advisable*, because the person might not want a bird for a pet

8.____

9. While temporarily assigned to switchboard duty, you receive a call from a man who says his uncle in Pittsburgh has just called him and threatened to commit suicide. The man is convinced his uncle intends to carry out his threat.
    Of the following, you should
    A. advise the man to have neighbors of the uncle check to see if the uncle is all right
    B. politely inform the man that such out-of-town incidents are beyond the authority of the local precinct
    C. take the uncle's name, address, and telephone number and immediately contact police authorities in Pittsburgh
    D. get the man's name, address, and telephone number so that you can determine whether the call is a hoax

9.____

10. Assume that in the course of your assigned duties you have just taken a necessary action which you feel has angered a citizen. After he has gone, you suddenly realize that the incident might result in an unjustified complaint.
    The MOST advisable action for you to take now would be to
    A. contact the person and apologize to him
    B. make complete notes on the incident and on any witnesses who might be helpful
    C. ask your superior what you might expect in case of such a complaint, without giving any hint of the actual occurrence
    D. accept the situation as one of the hazards of your job

10.____

11. Your job may bring you in contact with people from the community who are confronted with emergencies,, and are experiencing feelings of tension, anxiety, or even hostility. It is good to keep in mind what attitude is most helpful to people who, in such situations like these.
    Which of the following would be BEST to do?
    A. Present similar examples of your own problems to make the person feel that his problems are not unusual.
    B. Recognize the person's feelings, present information on available services, and make suggestions as to proper procedures

11.____

C. Expect that some of the information is exaggerated and encourage the person to let some time pass before seeking further help.
D. Have the person wait while you try to make arrangements for his problem to be solved.

12. Suppose that while on duty you receive a call from the owner of a gas station which is located within the precinct. The owner is annoyed with a certain rule made by the Police Department which concerns the operation of such stations. You agree with him.
Of the following, the BEST action for you to take is to
    A. make a report on the call and suggest to the owner that he write a letter to the Department about the rule
    B. tell the owner that there is little that can be done since such rules are departmental policy
    C. tell the owner that you agree with his complaint and that you will write a memo of his call
    D. establish good relations with the owner by suggesting how to word a letter that will get action from the department

13. Suppose that you are working at the switchboard when a call comes in late at night from a woman who reports that her neighbors are having a very noisy party. She gives you her first name, surname, and address, and you ask her title is *Miss* or *Mrs*. She replies that her title is irrelevant to her complaint, and wants to know why you ask.
Of the following possible ways of handling this, which is BEST?
    A. Insist that the title is necessary for identification purposes
    B. Tell her that it is merely to find out what her marital status is
    C. Agree that the information is not necessary and ask her how she wants to be referred to
    D. Find out why she shows such a peculiar reaction to a request for harmless information

14. While covering an assignment on the switchboard, you receive a call from a young girl who tells you of rumored plans for a gang fight in her neighborhood. You should
    A. take down the information so that a patrol squad can investigate the area and possibly keep the fight from starting
    B. discourage the girl from becoming alarmed by reminding her that it is only a rumor
    C. realize that this is a teenager looking for attention, humor her, and dismiss the matter
    D. take down the information but tell the girl that you need concrete information, and not just rumors, to take any action on her call

15. The one of the following which would MOST likely lead to friction among police administrative aides in a unit would be for the supervisor in charge of the unit to
    A. defend the actions of the aides he supervises when discussing them with his own supervisor

B. get his men to work together as a team in completing the work of the unit
C. praise each of the aides he supervises *in confidence* as the best aide in the unit
D. consider the point of view of the aides he supervises when assigning unpleasant tasks

16. Suppose that a police administrative aide who had been transferred to your office from another unit in your Department because of difficulties with his supervisor has been placed under your supervision.
    The BEST course of action for you to take FIRST is to
    A. analyze the aide's past grievance to determine if the transfer was the best settlement of the problem
    B. advise him of the difficulties his former supervisor had with other employees and encourage him not to feel bad about the transfer
    C. warn him that you will not tolerate any nonsense and that he will be watched carefully while assigned to your unit
    D. instruct him in the duties he will be performing in your unit and make him feel *wanted* in his new position

16._____

17. In which of the following circumstances would it be MOST appropriate for you to use an impersonal style of writing rather than a personal style, which relies on the use of personal pronouns and other personal references?
    When writing a memorandum to
    A. give your opinion to an associate on the advisability of holding a weekly staff meeting
    B. furnish your superior with data justifying a proposed outlay of funds for new equipment
    C. give your version of an incident which resulted in a complaint by a citizen about your behavior
    D. support your request for a transfer to another division

17._____

18. A newly appointed supervisor should learn as much as possible about the backgrounds of his subordinates.
    The statement is generally CORRECT because
    A. effective handling of subordinates is based upon knowledge of their individual differences
    B. knowing their backgrounds assures they will be treated objectively, equally, and without favor
    C. some subordinates perform more efficiently under one supervisor than under another
    D subordinates have confidence in a supervisor who knows all about them

18._____

19. You have found it necessary, for valid reasons, to criticize the work of one of the female police administrative aides. She later comes to your desk and accuses you of criticizing her work because she is a woman.
    The BEST way for you to deal with this employee is to
    A. ask her to apologize, since you would never allow yourself to be guilty of his kind of discrimination

19._____

B. discuss her complaint with her, explaining again and at greater length the reason for your criticism
C. assure her you wish to be fair, and ask her to submit a written report to you on her complaint
D. apologize for hurting her feelings and promise that she will be left alone in the future

20. The following steps are recognized steps in teaching an employee a new skill:
   I. Demonstrate how to do the work
   II. Let the learner do the work himself
   III. Explain the nature and purpose of the work
   IV. Correct poor procedures by suggestion and demonstration
   The CORRECT order for these steps is
   A. III, II, IV, I   B. II, I, III, IV   C. III, I, II, IV   D. I, III, II, IV

21. Suppose you have arranged an interview with a subordinate to try to help him overcome a serious shortcoming in his technical work. While you do not intend to talk to him about his attitude, you have noticed that he seems to be suspicious and resentful of people in authority. You need a record of the points covered in the discussion since further interviews are likely to be necessary.
   Your BEST course would be to
   A. write a checklist of points you wish to discuss and carefully check the points off as the interview progresses
   B. know exactly how you wish to proceed, and then make written notes during the interview of your subordinate's comments
   C. frankly tell your subordinate that you are recording the talk on tape but place the recorder where it will not hinder discussion
   D. keep in mind what you wish to accomplish and make notes on the interview immediately after it is over

22. A police administrative aide has explained a complicated procedure to several subordinates. He has been talking clearly, allowing time for information to sink in. He has also encouraged questions. Yet, he still questions his subordinates after his explanation, with the obvious objective of finding out whether they completely understand the procedure.
   Under these circumstances, the action of the police administrative aide, in asking questions about the procedure, is
   A. *not advisable*, because subordinates who do not now know the procedure which has been explained so carefully can read and study it
   B. *not advisable*, because he endangers his relationship with his subordinates by insulting their intelligence
   C. *advisable*, because subordinate basically resent instructions and seldom give their full attention in a group situation
   D. *advisable*, because the answers to his questions help him to determine whether he has gained his objective

23. The most competent of the police administrative aides is a pleasant, intelligent young woman who breaks the rules of the Department by occasionally making long personal telephone calls during working hours. You have not talked to her up until now about this fault. However, the calls are beginning to increase, and you decide to deal directly with the problem.
The BEST way to approach the subject with her would be to
   A. review with her the history of her infractions of the rules
   B. point out that her conduct is not fair to the other workers
   C. tell her that her personal calls are excessive and discuss it with her
   D. warn her quietly that you intend to apply penalties if necessary

24. Assume that you are supervising eight male police administrative aides who do similar clerical work. A group of four of them work on each side of a row of files which can be moved without much trouble. You notice that in each group there is a clique of three aides, leaving one member isolated. The two isolated members are relative newcomers.
Your BEST course in such a case would be to
   A. ignore the situation because to concern yourself with informal social arrangements of your subordinates would distract you from more important matters
   B. ask each of the cliques to invite the isolated member in their working group to lunch with them from time to time
   C. tell each group that you cannot allow cliques to form as it is bad for the morale of the unit
   D. find an excuse to move the file cabinet to the side of the room and then move the desks of the two isolated members close together

25. Suppose that your supervisor, who has recently been promoted and transferred to your division, asks you to review a certain procedure with a view to its possible revision. You know that several years ago a sergeant made a lengthy and intensive report based on a similar review.
Which of the following would it be BEST for you to do FIRST?
   A. Ask your supervisor if he is aware of the previous report
   B. Read the sergeant's report before you begin work to see what bearing it has on your assignment
   C. Begin work on the review without reading his report so that you will have a fresh point of view
   D. Ask the sergeant to assist you in your review

26. Using form letters in business correspondence is LEAST effective when
   A. answering letters on a frequently recurring subject
   B. giving the same information to many addresses
   C. the recipient is only interested in the routing information contained in the form letter
   D. a reply must be keyed to the individual requirements of the intended reader

8 (#1)

27. From the viewpoint of an office administrator, the BEST of the following reasons for distributing the incoming mail before the beginning of the regular work day is that
    A. distribution can be handled quickly and most efficiently at that time
    B. distribution later in the day may be distracting to or interfering with other employees
    C. the employees who distribute the mail can then perform other tasks during the rest of the day
    D. office activities for the day based on the mail may then be started promptly

27._____

28. Suppose you have had difficulty locating a document in the files because you could not decide where it should have been filed. You learn that other people in the office have had the same problem. You know that the document will be needed from time to time in the future.
    Your BEST course, when refiling the document, would be to
    A. make a written note of where you found it so that you will find it more easily the next time
    B. reclassify it and file it in the file where you first looked for it
    C. file it where you found it and put cross-reference sheets in the other likely files
    D. make a mental association to help you find it the next time and put it back where you found it

28._____

29. Suppose that your supervisor is attending a series of meetings of police captains in Philadelphia and will not be back until next Wednesday. He has left no instructions with you as to how you should handle telephone calls for him.
    In most instances, your BEST course of action would be to say:
    A. He isn't here just now.
    B. He is out of town and won't be back until next Wednesday.
    C. He won't be in today.
    D. He is in Philadelphia attending a meeting of police captains.

29._____

30. The one of the following which is USUALLY an important by-product of the preparation of a procedure manual is that
    A. information uncovered in the process of preparation may lead to improvement of procedures
    B. workers refer to the manual instead of bothering their supervisors for information
    C. supervisors use the manual for training stenographers
    D. employees have equal access to information needed to do their jobs

30._____

31. You have been asked to organize a clerical job and supervise police administrative aides who will do the actual work. The job consists of removing, from several boxes of data processing cards which are arranged in alphabetical order, the cards of those whose names appear on certain lists. The person removing the card then notes a date on the card. Assume that the work will be done accurately whatever system is used.

31._____

Which of the following statements describes both the MOST efficient method
and the BEST reasons for using that method? Have
- A. two aides work together, one calling names and the other extracting cards, and dating them, because the average production of any two aides working together should be higher, under these circumstances, than that of any two aides working alone
- B. each aide work alone, because it is easier to check spelling when reading the names than when listening to them
- C. two aides work together, one calling names and the other extracting cards and dating them, because social interaction tends to make work go faster
- D. each aide work alone, because the average production of any two aides, each working alone, should be higher, under these circumstances, than that of any two aides working together

32. The term *work flow*, when used in connection with office management or the activities in an office GENERALLY means the 32.____
    - A. rate of speed at which work flows through a single section of an office
    - B. use of charts in the analysis of various office functions
    - C. number of individual work units which can be produced by the average employee
    - D. step-by-step physical routing of work through its various procedures

Questions 33-40.

DIRECTIONS: Name of Offense   V A N D S B R U G H
Code Letter   c o m p l e x i t y
File Number   1 2 3 4 5 6 7 8 9 0

Assume that each of the above capital letters is the first letter of the name of an offense, that the small letter directly beneath each capita letter is the code letter for the offense, and that the number directly beneath each code letter is the file number for the offense.
In each of Questions 33 through 40, the code letters and file numbers should correspond to the capital letters.
If there is an error only in Column 2, mark your answer A.
If there is an error only in Column 3, mark your answer B.
If there is an error in both Column 2 and Column, mark your answer C.
If both Columns 2 and 3 are correct, mark your answer D.

Sample Questions:

COLUMN 1	COLUMN 2	COLUMN 3
BNARGHSVVU	emoxtylcci	6357905118

The code letters in Column 2 are correct, but the first 5 in Column 3 should be 2. Therefore, the answer is B.

	COLUMN 1	COLUMN 2	COLUMN 3	
33.	HGDSBNBSVR	ytplxmelcx	0945736517	33._____

34. SDGUUNHVAH   lptiimycoy   5498830120   34.____
35. BRSNAAVUDU   exlmooctpi   6753221848   35.____
36. VSRUDNADUS   cleipmopil   1568432485   36.____
37. NDSHVRBUAG   mplycxeiot   3450175829   37.____
38. GHUSNVBRDA   tyilmcexpo   9805316742   38.____
39. DBSHVURANG   pesycixomt   4650187239   39.____
40. RHNNASBDGU   xymnolepti   7033256398   40.____

KEY (CORRECT ANSWERS)

1.	B	11.	B	21.	D	31.	D
2.	A	12.	A	22.	D	32.	D
3.	D	13.	C	23.	C	33.	C
4.	B	14.	A	24.	D	34.	D
5.	D	15.	C	25.	A	35.	A
6.	A	16.	D	26.	D	36.	C
7.	D	17.	B	27.	D	37.	B
8.	C	18.	A	28.	C	38.	D
9.	C	19.	B	29.	B	39.	A
10.	B	20.	C	30.	A	40.	C

EXAMINATION SECTION
TEST 1

DIRECTIONS: Each question or incomplete statement is followed by several suggested answers or completions. Select the one that BEST answers the question or completes the statement. *PRINT THE LETTER OF THE CORRECT ANSWER IN THE SPACE AT THE RIGHT.*

1. You are operating the switchboard and you receive an outside call for an extension line which is busy.
   The one of the following which you should do FIRST is to
   A. ask the caller to try again later
   B. ask the caller to wait and inform him every thirty seconds about the status of the extension line
   C. tell the caller the line is busy and ask him if he wishes to wait
   D. tell the caller the line is busy and that you will connect him as soon as possible

   1.____

2. A person comes to your work area. He makes comments which make no sense, gives foolish opinions, and tells you that he has enemies who are after him. He appears to be mentally ill.
   Of the following, the FIRST action to take is to
   A. humor him by agreeing and sympathize with him
   B. try to reason with him and point out that his fears or opinions are unfounded
   C. have him arrested immediately
   D. tell him to leave at once

   2.____

3. You are speaking with someone on the telephone who asks you a question which you cannot answer. You estimate that you can probably obtain the requested information in about five minutes.
   Of the following, the MOST appropriate course of action would be to tell the caller that
   A. the information will take a short while to obtain, and then ask her for her name and number so that you can call her back when you have the information
   B. the information is available now, but she should call back later
   C. you do not know the answer and refer her to another division you think might be of service
   D. she is being placed on *hold* and that you will be with her in about five minutes

   3.____

4. A person with a very heavy foreign accent comes to your work area and starts talking to you. He is very excited and is speaking too rapidly for you to understand what he is saying.
   Of the following, the FIRST action for you to take is to

   4.____

21

A. refer the person to your supervisor
B. continue your work and ignore the person in the hope that he will be discouraged and leave the building
C. ask or motion to the person to speak more slowly and have him repeat what he is trying to communicate
D. assume that the person is making a complaint, tell him that his problem will be taken care of, and then go back to your work

5. Assume that you are responsible for handling supplies. You notice that you are running low on a particular type of manila file folder exceptionally fast. You believe that someone in the precinct is taking the folders for other than official use.
In this situation, the one of the following that you should do FIRST is to
A. put up a notice stating that supplies have been disappearing and ask for the staff's cooperation in eliminating the problem
B. speak to your supervisor about the matter and let him decide on a course of action
C. watch the supply cabinet to determine who is taking the folders
D. ignore the situation and put in a requisition for additional folders

6. One afternoon, several of the officers ask you to perform different tasks. Each task requires a half day of work. Each officer tells you that his assignment must be finished by 4 P.M. the next day.
Of the following, the BEST way to handle this situation is to
A. do the assignments as quickly as you can, in the order in which the officers handed them to you
B. do some work on each assignment in the order of the ranks of the assigning officers and hand in as much as you are able to finish
C. speak to your immediate supervisor in order to determine the priority of assignments
D. accept all four assignments but explain to the last officer that you may not be able to finish his job

7. Every morning, several officers congregate around your work station during their breaks. You find their conversations very distracting.
The one of the following which you should do FIRST is to
A. ask them to cooperate with you by taking their breaks somewhere else
B. concentrate as best you can because their breaks do not last very long
C. reschedule your break to coincide with theirs
D. tell your supervisor that the officers are very uncooperative

8. One evening when you are very busy, you answer the phone and find that you are speaking with one of the neighborhood cranks, an elderly man who constantly complains that his neighbors are noisy.
In this situation, the MOST appropriate action for you to take is to
A. hang up and go on with your work
B. note the complaint and process it in the usual way
C. tell the man that his complaint will be investigated and then forget about it
D. tell the man that you are very buy and ask him to call back later

3 (#1)

9. One morning you answer a telephone call for Lieutenant Jones, who is busy on another line. You inform the caller that Lieutenant Jones is on another line and this party says he will hold. After two minutes, Lieutenant Jones is still speaking on the first call.
Of the following, the FIRST thing for you to do is to
   A. ask the second caller whether it is an emergency
   B. signal Lieutenant Jones to let him know there is another call waiting for him
   C. request that the second caller try again later
   D. inform the second caller that Lieutenant Jones' line is still busy

9.____

10. The files in your office have been overcrowded and difficult to work with since you started working there. One day your supervisor is transferred and another aide in your office decides to discard three drawers of the oldest materials.
For him to take this action is
   A. *desirable*; it will facilitate handling the more active materials
   B. *undesirable*; no file should be removed from its point of origin
   C. *desirable*; there is no need to burden a new supervisor with unnecessary information
   D. *undesirable*; no file should be discarded without first noting what material has been discarded

10.____

11. You have been criticized by the lieutenant-in-charge because of spelling errors in some of your typing. You have only copied the reports as written, and you realize that the errors occurred in work given to you by Sergeant X.
Of the following, the BEST way for you to handle this situation is to
   A. tell the lieutenant that the spelling errors are Sergeant X's, not yours, because they occur only when you type his reports
   B. tell the lieutenant that you only type the reports as given to you, without implicating anyone
   C. inform Sergeant X that you have been unjustly criticized because of his spelling errors and politely request that he be more careful in the future
   D. use a dictionary whenever you have doubt regarding spelling

11.____

12. You have recently found several items misfiled. You believe that this occurred because a new administrative aide in your section has been making mistakes.
The BEST course of action for you to take is to
   A. refile the material and say nothing about it
   B. send your supervisor an anonymous note of complaint about the filing errors
   C. show the errors to the new administrative aide and tell him why they are errors in filing
   D. tell your supervisor that the new administrative aide makes a lot of errors in filing

12.____

13. One of your duties is to record information on a standard printed form regarding missing cars. One call you receive concerns a custom-built auto which has apparently been stolen. There seems to be no place on the form for many of the details which the owner gives you.

13.____

Of the following, the BEST way for you to obtain an adequate description of this car would be to
- A. complete the form as best you can and attach another sheet containing the additional information the owner gives you
- B. complete the form as best you can and request that the owner submit a photograph of the missing car
- C. scrap the form since it is inadequate in this case and make out a report based on the information the owner gives you
- D. complete the form as best you can and ignore extraneous information that the form does not call for

14. One weekend, you develop a painful infection in one hand. You know that your typing speed will be much slower than normal, and the likelihood of your making mistakes will be increased.
    Of the following, the BEST course of action for you to take in this situation is to
    - A. report to work as scheduled and do your typing assignments as best you can without complaining
    - B. report to work as scheduled and ask your co-workers to divide your typing assignments until your hand heals
    - C. report to work as scheduled and ask your supervisor for non-typing assignments until your hand heals
    - D. call in sick and remain on medical leave until your hand is completely healed so that you can perform your normal duties

15. When filling out a departmental form during an interview concerning a citizen complaint, an administrative aide should know the purpose of each question that he asks the citizen.
    For such information to be supplied by the department is
    - A. *advisable*, because the aide may lose interest in the job if he is not fully informed about the questions he has to ask
    - B. *inadvisable*, because the aide may reveal the true purpose of the questions to the citizens
    - C. *advisable*, because the aide might otherwise record superficial or inadequate answers if he does not fully understand the questions
    - D. *inadvisable*, because the information obtained through the form may be of little importance to the aide

16. Which one of the following is NOT a general accepted rule of telephone etiquette for an administrative aide?
    - A. Answer the telephone as soon as possible after the first ring
    - B. Speak in a louder than normal tone of voice, on the assumption that the caller is hard-of-hearing
    - C. Have a pencil and paper ready at all times with which to make notes and take messages
    - D. Use the tone of your voice to give the caller the impression of cooperativeness and willingness to be of service

17. The one of the following which is the BEST reason for placing the date and time of receipt of incoming mail is that this procedure
    A. aids the filing of correspondence in alphabetical order
    B. fixes responsibility for promptness in answering correspondence
    C. indicates that the mail has been checked for the presence of a return address
    D. makes it easier to distribute the mail in sequence

17.____

18. Which one of the following is the FIRST step that you should take when filing a document by subject?
    A. Arrange related documents by date with the latest date in front
    B. Check whether the document has been released for filing
    C. Cross-reference the document if necessary
    D. Determine the category under which the document will be filed

18.____

19. The one of the following which is NOT generally employed to keep tract of frequently used material requiring future attention is a
    A. card tickler file   B. dated follow-up folder
    C. periodic transferral of records   D. signal folder

19.____

20. Assume that a newly appointed administrative aide arrives 15 minutes late for the start of his tour of duty. One of his co-workers tells him not to worry because he has signed him in on time. The co-worker assures him that he would be willing to over for him anytime he is late and hopes the aide will do the same for him. The aide agrees to do so.
    This arrangement is
    A. *desirable*; it prevents both men from getting a record for tardiness
    B. *undesirable*; signing in for each other is dishonest
    C. *desirable*; cooperation among co-workers is an important factor in morale
    D. *undesirable*; they will get caught if one is held up in a lengthy delay

20.____

21. An administrative aide takes great pains to help a citizen who approaches him with a problem. The citizen thanks the aide curtly and without enthusiasm. Under these circumstances, it would be MOST courteous for the aide to
    A. tell the citizen he was glad to be of service
    B. ask the citizen to put the compliment into writing and send it to his supervisor
    C. tell the citizen just what pains he took to render this service so that the citizen will be fully aware of his efforts
    D. make no reply and ignore the citizen's remarks

21.____

22. Assume that your supervisor spends a week training you, a newly appointed administrative aide, to sort fingerprint for filing purposes. After doing this type of filing for several day, you get an idea which you believe would improve upon the method in use.
    Of the following, the BEST action for you to take in this situation is to
    A. wait to see whether your idea still look good after you have had more experience
    B. try your idea out before bringing it up with your supervisor

22.____

25

C. discuss your idea with your supervisor
D. forget about this idea since the fingerprint sorting system was devised by experts

23. Which one of the following is NOT a useful filing practice? 23.____
    A. Filing active records in the most accessible parts of the file cabinet
    B. Filling a file drawer to capacity in order to save space
    C. Gluing small documents to standard-size paper before filing
    D. Using different colored tab for various filing categories

24. A citizen comes in to make a complaint to an administrative aide. 24.____
    The one of the following action which would be the MOST serious example of discourtesy would be for the aide to
    A. refuse to look up from his desk even though he knows someone is waiting to speak to him
    B. not use the citizen's name when addressing him once his identity has been ascertained
    C. interrupt the citizen's story to ask questions
    D. listen to the complaint and refer the citizen to a special office

25. Suppose that one of your neighbors walks into the precinct where you are an administrative aide and asks you to make 100 copies of a letter on the office duplicating machine for his personal use. 25.____
    Of the following, what action should you take FIRST in this situation?
    A. Pretend that you do not know the person and order him to leave the building
    B. Call a police officer and report the person for attempting to make illegal use of police equipment
    C. Tell the person that you will copy the letter but only when you are off-duty
    D. Explain to the person that you cannot use police equipment for non-police work

KEY (CORRECT ANSWERS)

1. C
2. A
3. A
4. C
5. B

6. C
7. A
8. B
9. D
10. D

11. D
12. C
13. A
14. C
15. C

16. B
17. B
18. B
19. C
20. B

21. A
22. C
23. B
24. A
25. D

TEST 2

DIRECTIONS: Each question or incomplete statement is followed by several suggested answers or completions. Select the one that BEST answers the question or completes the statement. *PRINT THE LETTER OF THE CORRECT ANSWER IN THE SPACE AT THE RIGHT.*

Questions 1-6.

DIRECTIONS: Questions 1 through 6 are to be answered on the basis of the information supplied in the chart below.

LAW ENFORCEMENT OFFICERS KILLED
(By Type of Activity)
2012-2021

2012-2016
2017-2021

Activity	2012-2016	2017-2021
RESPONDING TO DISTURBANCE CALLS	48	50
BURGLARIES IN PROGRESS OR PURSUING BURGLARY SUSPECT	28	25
ROBBERIES IN PROGRESS OR PURSUING ROBBERY SUSPECT	48	74
ATTEMPTING OTHER ARRESTS	56	112
CIVIL DISORDERS	2	8
HANDLING, TRANSPORTING, CUSTODY OF PRISONERS	12	17
INVESTIGATING SUSPICIOUS PERSONS AND CIRCUMSTANCES	28	29
AMBUSH	13	29
UNPROVOKED MENTALLY DERANGED	5	20
TRAFFIC STOPS	10	19

1. According to the above chart, the percent of the total number of law enforcement officers killed from 2012-2021 in activities related to burglaries and robberies is MOST NEARLY _____ percent.
   A. 8.4   B. 19.3   C. 27.6   D. 36.2

1.____

2 (#2)

2. According to the above chart, the two of the following categories which increased from 2012–16 to 2017–21 by the same percent are
   A. ambush and traffic stops
   B. attempting other arrests and ambush
   C. civil disorders and unprovoked mentally deranged
   D. response to disturbance calls and investigating suspicious persons and circumstances

2.____

3. According to the above chart, the percentage increase in law enforcement officers killed from the 2012-16 period to the 2017-21 period is MOST NEARLY _____ percent.
   A. 34   B. 53   C. 65   D. 100

3.____

4. According to the above chart, in which one of the following activities did the number of law enforcement officers killed increase by 100 percent?
   A. Ambush
   B. Attempting other arrests
   C. Robberies in progress or pursuing robbery suspect
   D. Traffic stops

4.____

5. According to the above chart, the two of the following activities during which the total number of law enforcement officers killed from 2012 to 2021 was the same are
   A. burglaries in progress or pursuing burglary suspect and investigating suspicious persons and circumstances
   B. handling, transporting, custody of prisoner and traffic stops
   C. investigating suspicious persons and circumstances and ambush
   D. responding to disturbance calls and robberies in progress or pursuing robbery suspect

5.____

6. According to the categories in the above chart, the one of the following statements which can be made about law enforcement officers killed from 2012 to 2016 is that
   A. the number of law enforcement officers killed during civil disorders equals one-sixth of the number killed responding to disturbance calls
   B. the number of law enforcement officers killed during robberies in progress or pursuing robbery suspect equals 25 percent of the number killed while handling or transporting prisoners
   C. the number of law enforcement officers killed during traffic stops equals one-half the number killed for unprovoked reasons or by the mentally deranged
   D. twice as many law enforcement officers were killed attempting other arrests as were killed during burglaries in progress or pursuing burglary suspect

6.____

Questions 7-10.

DIRECTIONS: Assume that all arrests fall into two mutually exclusive categories, felonies and misdemeanors. Last week 620 arrests were made in Precinct A, of which 403 were for felonies. Questions 7 through 10 are to be answered on the basis of this information.

7. The percent of all arrests made in Precinct A last week which were for felonies was _____ percent.
   A. 55   B. 60   C. 65   D. 70

8. If 3/5 of all persons arrested for felonies and 1/4 of all persons arrested for misdemeanors were carrying weapons, then the number of arrests involving persons carrying weapons in Precinct A last week was MOST NEARLY
   A. 135   B. 295   C. 415   D. 525

9. If five times as many men as women were arrested for felonies, and half as many women as men were arrested for misdemeanors, then the number of women arrested in Precinct A last week was APPROXIMATELY
   A. 90   B. 120   C. 175   D. 210

10. If the ratio of arrests made on weekends (Friday through Sunday) to arrests made on weekdays (Monday through Thursday) is 2:1, then the number of arrests made in Precinct A last weekend was
    A. 308   B. 340   C. 372   D. 413

11. The police precincts covering the county receive calls at the average rate of two per minute during the 8 A.M. to 4 P.M. tour, but this rate increases by 50 percent during the 4 P.M. to 12 A.M. tour. However, the initial rate decreases by 50 percent during the 12 A.M. to 8 A.M. tour.
    The number of calls received by the precincts covering the county on this basis is one 24-hour day is
    A. 960   B. 1,440 C. 2,880 D. 3,360

12. If an administrative aide is expected to handle 15 calls per hour and Precinct C averages 840 calls during the 4 P.M. to 12 A.M. tour, then the number of aides needed in Precinct C to handle calls during this tour is
    A. 4   B. 5   C. 6   D. 7

13. If in a group of ten administrative aides, four type 40 words per minute, one types 45, two type 50, two type 60, and one types 65, then the average speed in the group is
    A. 49   B. 50   C. 51   D. 52

14. An administrative aide works from midnight to 8 A.M. on a certain day and then is off for 64 hours.
    He is due back at work at
    A. 8 A.M.   B. 12 noon   C. 4 P.M.   D. 12 midnight

15. If a certain aide take one hour to type 2 accident reports or 6 missing person reports, then the length of time he will require to finish 7 accident reports and 15 missing persons reports is _____ hours _____ minutes. 15._____
    A. 6; 0   B. 6; 30   C. 8; 0   D. 8; 40

16. If one administrative aide can alphabetize 320 reports per hour and another can do 280 per hour, then the number of reports that both could alphabetize during an 8-hour tour is 16._____
    A. 4,800   B. 5,200   C. 5,400   D. 5,700

17. If 1,000 candidates applied for administrative aide, and out of those applying 7/8 appear for the written test, and out of those who take the written test 66 2/4 percent pass it, and out of those who pass the written test 85 percent pass the medical exam, then the number of candidates still eligible to become administrative aides will be about 17._____
    A. 245   B. 495   C. 585   D. 745

18. If the number of murders in the city in 2018 was 415, and the number of murders has increased by 8 percent each year since that year, then in 2021 we would expect the number of murders to be about 18._____
    A. 484   B. 523   C. 548   D. 565

19. If a person reported missing on April 15 was found murdered on July 4, how many days was he missing? (Include April 15 but NOT July 4 in the total.) 19._____
    A. 76   B. 80   C. 82   D. 84

20. Suppose that a pile of 96 file cards measures one inch in height and that it takes you ½ hour to file these cards away. 20._____
    If you are given three piles of cards which measure 2½ inches high, 1¾ inches high, and 3³/₈ inches high, respectfully, the time it would take to file the cards is MOST NEARLY _____ hours and _____ minutes.
    A. 2; 30   B. 3; 50   C. 6; 45   D. 8; 15

Questions 21-30.

DIRECTIONS: Questions 21 through 30 test how good you are at catching mistakes in typing or printing. In each question, the name and addresses in Column II should be an exact copy of the name and address in Column I.
Mark your answer:
A. if there is no mistake in either name or address
B. if there is a mistake in both name and address
C. if there is a mistake only in the name
D. if there is a mistake only in the address

COLUMN I   COLUMN II

21. Milos Yanocek   Milos Yanocek   21._____
    33-60 14 Street   33-60 14 Street
    Long Island City, NY 11011   Long Island City, NY 11001

22. Alphonse Sabattelo   Alphonse Sabbattelo   22._____
     24 Minnetta Lane   24 Minetta Lane
     New York, NY 10006   New York, NY 10006

23. Helen Stearn   Helene Steam   23._____
     5 Metroplitan Oval   5 Metropolitan Oval
     Bronx, NY 10462   Bronx, NY 10462

24. Jacob Weisman   Jacob Weisman   24._____
     231 Francis Lewis Boulevard 231 Francis Lewis Boulevard
     Forest Hills, NY 11325   Forest Hill, NY 11325

25. Riccardo Fuente   Riccardo Fuentes   25._____
     135 West 83 Street   134 West 88 Street
     New York, NY 10024   New York, NY 10024

26. Dennis Lauber   Dennis Lauder   26._____
     52 Avenue D   52 Avenue D
     Brooklyn, NY 11216   Brooklyn, NY 11216

27. Paul Cutter   Paul Cutter   27._____
     195 Galloway Avenue   175 Galloway Avenue
     Staten Island, NY 10356   Staten Island, NY 10365

28. Sean Donnelly   Sean Donnelly   28._____
     45-58 41 Avenue   45-58 41 Avenue
     Woodside, NY 11168   Woodside, NY 11168

29. Clyde Willot   Clyde Willat   29._____
     1483 Rockaway Avenue   1483 Rockaway Avenue
     Brooklyn, NY 11238   Brooklyn, NY 11238

30. Michael Stanakis   Michael Stanakis   30._____
     419 Sheriden Avenue   419 Sheraden Avenue
     Staten Island, NY 10363   Staten Island, NY 10363

Questions 31-40.

DIRECTIONS: Questions 31 through 40 are to be answered SOLELY on the basis of the following information.

Column I consists of serial numbers of dollar bills. Column II shows different ways of arranging the corresponding serial numbers.

The serial numbers of dollar bills in Column I begin and end with a capital letter and have an eight-digit number in between. The serial numbers in Column I are to be arranged according to the following rules:

6 (#2)

First: In alphabetical order according to the first letter.
Second: When two or more serial numbers have the same first letter, in alphabetical order according to the last letter.
Third: When two or more serial numbers have the same first and last letters, in numerical order, beginning with the lowest number.

The serial numbers in Column I are numbered (1) through (5) in the order in which they are listed. In Column II, the numbers (1) through (5) are arranged in four different ways to show different arrangements of the corresponding serial numbers. Choose the answer in Column II in which the serial numbers are arranged according to the above rules.

SAMPLE QUESTION:

	COLUMN I		COLUMN II
(1)	E75044127B	(A)	4, 1, 3, 2, 5
(2)	B96399104A	(B)	4, 1 2, 3, 5
(3)	B93939086A	(C)	4, 3, 2 5, 1
(4)	B47064465H	(D)	3, 2, 5, 4, 1
(5)	B99040922A		

In the sample question, the four serial numbers starting with B should be put before the serial numbers starting with E. The serial numbers starting with B and ending with A should be put before the serial number starting with B and ending with H. The three serial numbers starting with B and ending with A should be listed in numerical order, beginning with the lowest number. The correct way to arrange the serial numbers, therefore, is

(3) B93939086A
(2) B96399104A
(5) B99040922A
(4) B47064465H
(1) B75044127B

Since the order of arrangement is 3, 2, 5, 4, 1, the answer to the sample question is (D).

		COLUMN I			COLUMN II	
31.	(1)	P44343324Y	A.	2, 3, 1, 4, 5		31.____
	(2)	P44141341S	B.	1, 5, 3, 2, 4		
	(3)	P44141431L	C.	4, 2, 3, 5, 1		
	(4)	P41143413W	D.	5, 3, 2, 4, 1		
	(5)	P44313433H				
32.	(1)	D89077275M	A.	3, 2, 5, 3, 1		32.____
	(2)	D98073724N	B.	1, 4, 3, 2, 5		
	(3)	D90877274N	C.	4, 1, 5, 2, 3		
	(4)	D98877275M	D.	1, 3, 2, 5, 3		
	(5)	D98873725N				

7 (#2)

33. (1) H32548137E   A. 2, 4, 5, 1, 3   33.____
    (2) H35243178A   B. 1, 5, 2, 3, 4
    (3) H35284378F   C. 1, 5, 2, 4, 3
    (4) H35288337A   D. 2, 1, 5, 3, 4
    (5) H32883173B

34. (1) K24165039H   A. 4, 2, 5, 3, 1   34.____
    (2) F24106599A   B. 2, 3, 4, 1, 5
    (3) L21406639G   C. 4, 2, 5, 1, 3
    (4) C24156093A   D. 1, 3, 4, 5, 2
    (5) K24165593D

35. (1) H79110642E   A. 2, 1, 3, 5, 4   35.____
    (2) H79101928E   B. 2, 1, 4, 5, 3
    (3) A79111567F   C. 3, 5, 2, 1, 4
    (4) H79111796E   D. 4, 3, 5, 1, 2
    (5) A79111618F

36. (1) P16388385W   A. 3, 4, 5, 2, 1   36.____
    (2) R16388335V   B. 2, 3, 4, 5, 1
    (3) P16383835W   C. 2, 4, 3, 1, 5
    (4) R18386865V   D. 3, 1, 5, 2, 4
    (5) P18686865W

37. (1) B42271749G   A. 4, 1, 5, 2, 3   37.____
    (2) B42271779G   B. 4, 1, 2, 5, 3
    (3) E43217779G   C. 1, 2, 4, 5, 3
    (4) B42874119C   D. 5, 3, 1, 2, 4
    (5) E42817749G

38. (1) M57906455S   A. 4, 1, 5, 3, 2   38.____
    (2) N87077758S   B. 3, 4, 1, 5, 2
    (3) N87707757B   C. 4, 1, 5, 2, 3
    (4) M57877759B   D. 1, 5, 3, 2, 4
    (5) M57906555S

39. (1) C69336894Y   A. 2, 5, 3, 1, 4   39.____
    (2) C69336684V   B. 3, 2, 5, 1, 4
    (3) C69366887W   C. 3, 1, 4, 5, 2
    (4) C69366994Y   D. 2, 5, 1, 3, 4
    (5) C69336865V

40. (1) A56247181D   A. 1, 5, 3, 2, 4   40.____
    (2) A56272128P   B. 3, 1, 5, 2, 4
    (3) H56247128D   C. 3, 2, 1, 5, 4
    (4) H56272288P   D. 1, 5, 2, 3, 4
    (5) A56247188D

Questions 41-48.

DIRECTIONS: Questions 41 through 48 are to be answered SOLELY on the basis of the following passage.

Auto theft is prevalent and costly. In 2020, 486,000 autos valued at over $500 million were stolen. About 28 percent of the inhabitants of federal prisons are there as a result of conviction of interstate auto theft under the Dyer Act. In California alone, auto thefts cost the criminal justice system approximately $60 million yearly.

The great majority of auto theft is for temporary use rather than resale, as evidenced by the fact that 88 percent of autos stolen in 2020 were recovered. In Los Angeles, 64 percent of stolen autos that were recovered were found within two days and about 80 percent within a week. Chicago reports that 71 percent of the recovered autos were found within four miles of the point of theft. The FBI estimates that 8 percent of stolen cars are taken for the purpose of stripping them for parts, 12 percent for resale, and 5 percent for use in another crime. Auto thefts are primarily juvenile acts. Although only 21 percent of all arrests for nontraffic offenses in 2020 were of individuals under 18 years of age, 63 percent of auto theft arrests were of persons under 18. Auto theft represents the start of many criminal careers; in an FBI sample of juvenile auto theft offenders, 41 percent had no prior arrest record.

41. In the above passage, the discussion of the reasons for auto theft does NOT include the percent of
    A. autos stolen by prior offenders
    B. recovered stolen autos found close to the point of theft
    C. stolen autos recovered within a week
    D. stolen autos which were recovered

42. Assuming the figures in the above passage remain constant, you may logically estimate the cost of auto thefts to the California criminal justice system over a five-year period beginning in 2020 to have been about _____ million.
    A. $200   B. $300   C. $440   D. $500

43. According to the above passage, the percent of stolen autos in Los Angeles which were not recovered within a week was _____ percent.
    A. 12   B. 20   C. 29   D. 36

44. According to the above passage, MOST auto thefts are committed by
    A. former inmates of federal prisons
    B. juveniles
    C. persons with a prior arrest record
    D. residents of large cities

45. According to the above passage, MOST autos are stolen for
    A. resale
    B. stripping of parts
    C. temporary use
    D. use in another crime

46. According to the above passage, the percent of persons arrested for auto theft who were under 18
 A. equals nearly the same percent of stolen autos which were recovered
 B. equals nearly two-thirds of the total number of persons arrested for nontraffic offenses
 C. is the same as the percent of persons arrested for nontraffic offenses who were under 18
 D. is three times the percent of persons arrested for nontraffic offenses who were under 18

46.____

47. An APPROPRIATE title for the above passage is
 A. How Criminal Careers Begin B. Recovery of Stolen Cars
 C. Some Statistics on Auto Theft D. The Costs of Auto Theft

47.____

48. Based on the above passage, the number of cars taken for use in another crime in 2020 was
 A. 24,300   B. 38,880   C. 48,600   D. 58,320

48.____

Questions 49-55.

DIRECTIONS: Questions 49 through 55 are to be answered SOLELY on the basis of the following passage.

Burglar alarms are designed to detect intrusion automatically. Robbery alarms enable a victim of a robbery or an attack to signal for help. Such devices can be located in elevators, hallways, homes and apartments, businesses and factories, and subways, as well as on the street in high-crime areas. Alarms could deter some potential criminals from attacking targets so protected. If alarms were prevalent and not visible, then they might serve to suppress crime generally. In addition, of course, the alarms can summon the police when they are needed.

All alarms must perform three functions: sensing or initiation of the signal, transmission of the signal, and annunciation of the alarm. A burglar alarm needs a sensor to detect human presence or activity in an unoccupied enclosed area like a building or a room. A robbery victim would initiate the alarm by closing a foot or wall switch, or by triggering a portable transmitter which would send the alarm signal to a remote receiver. The signal can sound locally as a loud noise to frighten away a criminal, or it can be sent silently by wire to a central agency. A centralized annunciator requires either private lines from each alarmed point, or the transmission of some information on the location of the signal.

49. A conclusion which follows LOGICALLY from the above passage is that
 A. burglar alarms employ sensor devices; robbery alarms make use of initiation devices
 B. robbery alarms signal intrusion without the help of the victim; burglar alarms require the victim to trigger a switch
 C. robbery alarms sound locally; burglar alarms are transmitted to a central agency
 D. the mechanisms for a burglar alarm and a robbery alarm are alike

49.____

50. According to the above passage, alarms can be located
    A. in a wide variety of settings
    B. only in enclosed areas
    C. at low cost in high-crime areas
    D. only in places where potential criminal will be deterred

50.____

51. According to the above passage, which of the following is ESSENTIAL if a signal is to be received in a central office?
    A. A foot or wall switch
    B. A noise producing mechanism
    C. A portable reception device
    D. Information regarding the location of the source

51.____

52. According to the above passage, an alarm system can function WITHOUT a
    A. centralized annunciating device
    B. device to stop the alarm
    C. sensing or initiating device
    D. transmission device

52.____

53. According to the above passage, the purpose of robbery alarms is to
    A. find out automatically whether a robbery has taken place
    B. lower the crime rate in high-crime areas
    C. make a loud noise to frighten away the criminal
    D. provide a victim with the means to signal for help

53.____

54. According to the above passage, alarms might aid in lessening crime if they were
    A. answered promptly by police
    B. completely automatic
    C. easily accessible to victims
    D. hidden and widespread

54.____

55. Of the following, the BEST title for the above passage is
    A. Detection of Crime By Alarms
    B. Lowering the Crime Rate
    C. Suppression of Crime
    D. The Prevention of Robbery

55.____

KEY (CORRECT ANSWERS)

1. C	11. C	21. D	31. D	41. A	51. D
2. C	12. D	22. B	32. B	42. B	52. A
3. B	13. A	23. C	33. A	43. B	53. D
4. B	14. D	24. A	34. C	44. B	54. D
5. B	15. A	25. B	35. C	45. C	55. A
6. D	16. A	26. C	36. D	46. D	
7. C	17. B	27. D	37. B	47. C	
8. B	18. B	28. A	38. A	48. A	
9. C	19. B	29. B	39. A	49. A	
10. D	20. B	30. D	40. D	50. A	

EXAMINATION SECTION
TEST 1

DIRECTIONS: Each question or incomplete statement is followed by several suggested answers or completions. Select the one that BEST answers the question or completes the statement. *PRINT THE LETTER OF THE CORRECT ANSWER IN THE SPACE AT THE RIGHT.*

1. As an administrative aide, it is your job to type reports prepared by several police officers. These reports are then returned to them for review and signature. Officer X consistently submits reports to you which contain misspellings and incorrect punctuation.
   Of the following, the BEST action for you to take is to
   A. tell your supervisor that something must be done about Officer X's poor English
   B. ask Officer X for permission to correct any mistakes
   C. assemble all of the officers and tell them that you refuse to correct their mistakes
   D. tell Officer X to be more careful

1._____

2. On a chart used in your precinct, there appear small figures of men, women, and children to denote population trends. Your supervisor assigns you to suggest possible symbols for a char which will be used to indicate daily vehicular traffic flow in the area covered by this precinct.
   In this situation, your BEST course of action would be to
   A. tell your supervisor an artist should be hired to draw these symbols
   B. make up a list of possible symbols, such as cars and trucks
   C. say that any decision as to the symbols to be used should be made at a higher level
   D. find out how many vehicles use the area

2._____

3. As an administrative aide, you are assigned to the telephone switchboard. An extremely irate citizen calls complaining in bigoted terms about a group of Black teenagers who congregate in front of his house. The caller insists on speaking to whoever is in charge. At the moment, Sergeant X, a black man, is in charge.
   The BEST course of action for you to take is to
   A. inform the caller that the teenagers may meet wherever they wish
   B. tell the caller that Sergeant X, a black man, is in charge, and ask him to call back later when a white man will be there
   C. tell the caller that you resent his bigotry and insist that he call back when he has calmed down
   D. acquaint Sergeant X with the circumstances and connect the caller with him

3._____

4. Assume that you have access to restricted materials such as conviction records. A friend asks you, unofficially, if a man he has recently met has a record of conviction.
The BEST thing for you to do is to
   A. give your friend the information he wants and inform your supervisor of your actions
   B. tell your friend that you are not allowed to give out such information
   C. tell your friend you will try to get the information for him but do not take any action
   D. give him the information because it is a matter of public record

4.____

5. Assume that you are an administrative aide assigned to a busy telephone information center.
Of the following, which is the MOST important technique to use when answering the telephone?
   A. Using many technical police terms
   B. Speaking slowly, in a monotone, for clarity
   C. Using formal English grammar
   D. Speaking clearly and distinctly

5.____

6. As an administrative aide, you are asked by an officer working in an adjacent office to type a very important letter without mistakes or corrections exactly as he has prepared it. As you are typing, you notice a word which, according to the dictionary, is misspelled.
Under the circumstances, you should
   A. ignore the error and type it exactly as prepared
   B. change the spelling without telling the officer
   C. ask the officer if you should change the spelling
   D. change the spelling and tell the officer

6.____

7. As am administrative aide, you are in charge of a large complex of files. In an effort to be helpful, some officers who frequently use the file have begun to refile material they had been using. Unfortunately, they often make errors.
Of the following, your BEST course of action is to
   A. ask them to leave the files for you to put away
   B. ask your supervisor to reprimand them
   C. frequently check the whole filing system for errors
   D. tell them they are making mistakes and insist they leave the files alone

7.____

8. One afternoon several of the police officers ask you to do different tasks. Each task will take about a day to complete, but each officer insists that his work must be completed immediately.
Your BEST course of action is to
   A. do a little of each assignment given to you
   B. ask your fellow workers to help you with the assignment
   C. speak to your supervisor in order to determine the priority of the assignments
   D. do the work in the order of the rank of the officers giving the assignments

8.____

Questions 9-12.

DIRECTIONS: Questions 9 through 12 are to be answered on the basis of the following passage.

It should be emphasized that one goal of law enforcement is the reduction of stress between one population group and another. When no stress exists between populations, law enforcement can deal with other tensions or simply perform traditional police functions. However, when stress between populations does exist, law enforcement, in its efforts to prevent disruptive behavior, becomes committed to reducing that stress (if for no other reason than its responsibility to maintain an orderly environment). The type of stress to be reduced, unlike the tension stemming from social change, is stress generated through intergroup and interracial friction. Of course, all sources of tension are inextricably interrelated, but friction between different populations in the community is of immediate concern to law enforcement.

9. The above passage emphasizes that, during times of stress between groups in the community, it is necessary for the police to attempt to
   A. continue their traditional duties
   B. eliminate tension resulting from social change
   C. reduce intergroup stress
   D. punish disruptive behavior

10. Based on the above passage, police concern with tension among groups in a community is MOST likely to stem primarily from their desire to
   A. establish racial justice   B. prevent violence
   C. protect property   D. unite the diverse groups

11. According to the above passage, enforcers of the law are responsible for
   A. analyzing consequences of population-group hostility
   B. assisting social work activities
   C. creating order in the environment
   D. explaining group behavior

12. The factor which produces the tension accompanying social change is
   A. a disorderly environment
   B. disruptive behavior
   C. inter-community hostility
   D. not discussed in the above passage

Questions 13-19.

DIRECTIONS: Questions 13 through 19 are to be answered on the basis of the information given in the following passage.

From a nationwide point of view, the need for new housing units during the years immediately ahead will be determined by four major factors. The most important factor is the net change in household formations—that is, the difference between the number of new households that are formed and the number of existing households that are dissolved, whether by death or other circumstances. During the 1990's, as the children born during the decades of the 60's and 70's come of age and marry, the total number of households is expected to increase at a rate of more than 1,000,000 annually. The second factor affecting the need for new housing units is *removals*—that is, existing units that are demolished, damaged beyond repair, or otherwise removed from the housing supply. A third factor is the number of existing vacancies. To some extent, vacancies can satisfy the housing demand caused by increases in total number of households or by removals, although population shifts that are already under way mean that some areas will have a surfeit of vacancies and other areas will be faced with serious shortages of housing. A final factor, and one that has only recently assumed major importance, is the increasing demand for second homes. These may take any form from a shack in the woods for the city dweller to a *pied-a-terre* in the city for a suburbanite. Whatever the form, however, it is certain that increasing leisure time, rising amounts of discretionary income, and improvements in transportation are leading more and more Americans to look on a second home not as a rich man's luxury but as the common man's right.

13. The above passage uses the term *housing units* to refer to
    A. residences of all kinds
    B. apartment buildings only
    C. one-family houses only
    D. the total number of families in the United States

14. The passage uses the word *removals* to mean
    A. the shift of population from one area to another
    B. vacancies that occur when families move
    C. financial losses suffered when a building is damaged or destroyed
    D. former dwellings that are demolished or can no longer be used for housing

15. The expression *pied-a-terre* appears in the next-to-last sentence in the passage. A person who is not familiar with the expression should be able to tell from the way it is used here that it probably means
    A. a suburban home owned by a commuter
    B. a shack in the woods
    C. a second home that is used from time to time
    D. overnight lodging for a traveler in a strange city

16. Of the factors described in the passage as having an important influence on the demand for housing, which factor—taken alone—is LEAST likely to encourage the construction of new housing?
    The
    A. net change in household formations
    B. destruction of existing housing
    C. existence of vacancies
    D. use of second homes

17. Based on the above passage, the TOTAL increase in the number of households during the 1990's is expected to be MOST NEARLY
    A. 1,000,000
    B. 10,000,000
    C. 100,000,000
    D. 1,000,000,000

18. Which one of the following conclusions could MOST logically be drawn from the information given in the passage?
    A. The population of the United States is increasing at the rate of about 1,000,000 people annually.
    B. There is already a severe housing shortage in all parts of the country.
    C. The need for additional housing units is greater in some parts of the country than in others.
    D. It is still true that only wealthy people can afford to keep up more than one home.

18.____

19. Which one of the following conclusions could NOT logically be drawn from the information given in the passage?
    A. The need for new housing will be even greater in the 2000's than in the 1990's.
    B. Demolition of existing housing must be taken into account in calculating the need for new housing construction.
    C. Having a second home is more common today than it was in the 1960's.
    D. Part of the housing needs of the 1990's can be met by vacancies.

19.____

20. You are making a report on the number of incoming calls handled by two different switchboards. Over a five-day period, the total count of incoming calls per day for both switchboards together was 2,773. The average number of incoming calls per day for Switchboard A was 301. You cannot find one day's tally for Switchboard B, but the total for the other four days for Switchboard B come to 1,032.
    Determine from this how many incoming calls must have been reported on the *missing* tally for Switchboard B.
    A. 236 B. 259 C. 408 D. 1,440

20.____

21. Assume that one-page notices for distribution may be reproduced by photocopy or by a designer. The cost for photocopying is 5½ cents per copy. It can also be reproduced by a designer for an initial preparation cost of $1.38 plus a per-copy cost of one cent.
    Strictly according to cost, which of the following is the LOWEST number of copies at which it would be more economical to choose the designer instead of photocopying?
    A. 15 B. 30 C. 45 D. 138

21.____

22. An employee completed 75% of a clerical assignment in four days.
    How much of it did he complete in the last two days if he finished 3/8 of it in the first two days?
    A. 1/4 B. 3/8 C. 5/8 D. 3/4

22.____

23. Seven hundred people are to be scheduled for interviews.
    If 58% of these 700 people have already been scheduled, how many more must be scheduled?
    A. 138 B. 294 C. 406 D. 410

23.____

24. In recent years, an average of 35% of the violations reported in any given month have been corrected by the time of a follow-up inspection one month later. Last month, 240 violations were reported, and this month's follow-up inspections show that 93 of them have been corrected.
How many more violations have been corrected than would have been expected based on the average rate?
   A. 5   B. 9   C. 33   D. 58

25. Suppose that, on a scaled drawing of an office floor plan, ½ inch equals 2 feet. An office that is actually 12 feet wide and 17 feet long has which of the following dimensions on this scaled drawing?
   _____ wide and _____.
   A. 3"; 4.25"   B. 6"' 8.5"   C. 12"; 17"   D. 24"; 34"

KEY (CORRECT ANSWERS)

1.	B	11.	C
2.	B	12.	D
3.	D	13.	A
4.	B	14.	D
5.	D	15.	C
6.	C	16.	C
7.	A	17.	B
8.	C	18.	C
9.	C	19.	A
10.	B	20.	A

21.	C
22.	B
23.	B
24.	B
25.	A

TEST 2

DIRECTIONS: Each question or incomplete statement is followed by several suggested answers or completions. Select the one that BEST answers the question or completes the statement. *PRINT THE LETTER OF THE CORRECT ANSWER IN THE SPACE AT THE RIGHT.*

1. Suppose that employees in a certain division put in a total of 1,250 hours of overtime in 2019. In 2020, total overtime hours for the same division were 2% less than in 2019, but in 2021 overtime hours increased by 8% over the 2020 total.
   How many overtime hours were worked by the staff of this division in 2021?
   A. 1,323   B. 1,331   C. 1,350   D. 1,375

   1.____

2. A particular operation currently involves 75 employees, 80% of whom work in the field and the rest of whom are office staff. A management study has shown that in order to be truly efficient, the operation should have a ratio of at least 1 office employee to every 3 field employees, and the study recommends that the number of field employees remain the same as at present.
   What is the MINIMUM number of employees needed to carry out the operation efficiently, according to this recommendation?
   A. 65   B. 75   C. 80   D. 100

   2.____

Questions 3-6.

DIRECTIONS: Questions 3 through 6 are to be answered on the basis of the information given in the following passage.

    Data processing is by no means a new invention. In one form or another, it has been carried on throughout the entire history of civilization. In its most general sense, data processing means organizing data so that it can be used for a specific purpose, a procedure commonly known simply as *record-keeping* or paperwork. With the development of modern office equipment, and particularly with the recent introduction of computers, the techniques of data processing have become highly elaborate and sophisticated, but the basic purpose remains the same: turning raw data into useful information.

    The key concept here is usefulness. The data, or input, that is to be processed can be compared to the raw material that is to go into a manufacturing process. The information, or output, that results from data processing—like the finished product of a manufacturer—should be clearly usable. A collection of data has little value unless it is converted into information that serves a specific function.

3. The expression *paperwork*, as it is used in this passage,
   A. shows that the author regards such operations as a waste of time
   B. has the same general meaning as *data processing*
   C. refers to methods of record-keeping that are no longer in use
   D. indicates that the public does not understand the purpose of data processing

   3.____

45

4. The passage indicates that the use of computers has
   A. greatly simplified the clerical work in an office
   B. led to more complicated systems for the handling of data
   C. had no effect whatsoever on data processing
   D. made other modern office machines obsolete

5. Which of the following BEST expresses the basic principle of data processing as it is described in the passage?
   A. Input – processing – output
   B. Historical record-keeping – modern techniques – specific functions
   C. Office equipment – computer – accurate data
   D. Raw material – manufacturer - retailer

6. According to the above passage, data processing may be described as
   A. a new management technique
   B. computer technology
   C. information output
   D. record-keeping

Questions 7-10.

DIRECTIONS: Questions 7 through 10 are to be answered on the basis of the following passage.

Analysis of current data reveals that motor vehicle transportation actually requires less space than was used for other types of transportation in the pre-automobile era, even including the substantial area taken by freeways. The reason is that when the fast-moving through traffic is put on built-for-the-purpose arterial roads, then the amount of ordinary space needed for strictly local movement and for access to property drops sharply. Even the amount of land taken for urban expressways turns out to be surprisingly small in terms either of total urban acreage or of the volume of traffic they carry. No existing or contemplated urban expressway system requires as much as 3 percent of the land in the areas it serves, and this would be exceptionally high. The Los Angeles freeway system, when complete, will occupy only 2 percent of the available land; the same is true of the District of Columbia, where only 0.75 percent will be pavement, with the remaining 1.25 percent as open space. California studies estimate that, in a typical California urban community, 1.6 to 2 percent of the area should be devoted to freeways, which will handle 50 to 60 percent of all traffic needs, and about ten times as much land to the ordinary roads and streets that carry the rest of the traffic. By comparison, when John A. Sutter laid out Sacramento in 1850, he provided 38 percent of the area for streets and sidewalks. The French architect, Pierre L'Enfant, proposed 59 percent of the area of the District of Columbia for roads and streets; urban renewal in Southwest Washington, incorporating a modern street network, reduced the acreage of space for pedestrian and vehicular traffic in the renewal area from 48.2 to 41.5 percent of the total. If we are to have a reasonable consideration of the impact of highway transportation on contemporary urban development, it would be well to understand these relationships.

7. The author of this passage says that
   A. modern transportation uses less space than was used for transportation before the auto age
   B. expressways require more space than streets in terms of urban acreage

C. typical urban communities were poorly designed in terms of relationship between space used for traffic and that used for other purposes
D. the need for local and access roads would increase if the number of expressways were increased

8. According to the above passage, it was originally planned that the percent of the area to be used for roads and streets in the District of Columbia should be MOST NEARLY
   A. 40%   B. 45%   C. 505   D. 60%

9. The above passage states that the amount of space needed for local traffic
   A. *increases* when arterial highways are constructed
   B. *decreases* when arterial highways are constructed
   C. *decreases* when there is more land available
   D. *increases* when there is more land available

10. According to the above passage, studies estimate that, in a typical California urban community, the amount of land devoted to ordinary roads and streets as compared with that devoted to freeways should be MOST NEARLY _____ as much.
    A. one-half   B. one-tenth   C. twice   D. ten times

Questions 11-13.

DIRECTIONS: Questions 11 through 13 are to be answered on the basis of the following passage.

A glaring exception to the usual practice of the judicial trial as a means of conflict resolution is the utilization of administrative hearings. The growing tendency to create administrative bodies with rule-making and quasi-judicial powers has shattered many standard concepts. A comprehensive examination of the legal process cannot neglect these newer patterns.

In the administrative process, the legislative, executive, and judicial functions are mixed together, and many functions, such as investigating, advocating, negotiating, testifying, rule-making an adjudicating, are carried out by the same agency. The reason for the breakdown of the separation-of-powers formula is not hard to find. It was felt by Congress, and state and municipal legislatures, that certain regulatory tasks could not be performed efficiently, rapidly, expertly, and with due concern for the public interest by the traditional branches of government. Accordingly, regulatory agencies were delegated powers to consider disputes from the earliest stage of investigation to the final stages of adjudication entirely within each agency itself, subject only to limited review in the regular courts.

11. The above passage states that the usual means for conflict resolution is through the use of
    A. judicial trial   B. administrative hearing
    C. legislation   D. regulatory agencies

12. The above passage *implies* that the use of administrative hearing in resolving conflict is a(n) _____ approach.
    A. traditional
    B. new
    C. dangerous
    D. experimental

13. The above passage states that the reason for the breakdown of the separation-of-powers formula in the administrative process is that
    A. Congress believed that certain regulatory tasks could be better performed by separate agencies
    B. legislative and executive functions are incompatible in the same agency
    C. investigative and regulatory functions are not normally reviewed by the courts
    D. state and municipal legislatures are more concerned with efficiency than with legality

14. An employee examining the summonses of individuals appearing for hearings noticed that the address on one summons was the same as that of an individual who had appeared earlier that day. He asked the second respondent if he knew the first respondent.
    The MOST appropriate evaluation of the employee's behavior is that he should
    A. not have mentioned any other respondent to the second respondent
    B. not waste time inspecting summonses in such detail
    C. be commended for inspecting summonses so carefully
    D. be commended for his investigation of the respondents

15. An employee is assigned to maintain all types of frequently used reference materials such as booklets and technical papers. He keeps these in a pile on a shelf in order of arrival. When new material arrives, he put it on top of the pile. Which of the following BEST evaluates the employee's handling of this reference material?
    His system is MOST likely to result in _____ filing and _____ retrieval.
    A. fast; slow   B. slow; slow   C. fast; fast   D. slow; fast

16. An employee computes statistics relating to proceeding. The method he devised consists of organizing his source and summary documents in such a manner that at any time another employee can assume the work. This method takes a little more time than other possible methods.
    Which of the following statements BEST evaluates the judgment of the employee in devising such a method?
    The employee has used
    A. *good* judgment because it is important to provide for continuity
    B. *poor* judgment because he is not using the fastest method
    C. *good* judgment because, if a job is done as fast as possible, it becomes tiring
    D. *poor* judgment because it is not an employee's responsibility to prepare for a replacement

5 (#2)

17. Assume that it is your job to receive incoming telephone calls. Those calls which you cannot handle yourself have to be transferred to the appropriate office.
If you receive an outside call for an extension line which is busy, the one of the following which you should do FIRST is to
    A. interrupt the person speaking on the extension and tell him a call is waiting
    B. tell the caller the line is busy and let him know every thirty seconds whether or not it is free
    C. leave the caller on *hold* until the extension is free
    D. tell the caller the line is busy and ask him if he wishes to wait

17._____

18. On one occasion in a certain office, an elderly employee collapsed, apparently the victim of a heart attack. Chaos broke out in the office as several people tried to help him and several others tried to get assistance.
Of the following, the MOST certain way of avoiding such chaos in the future is to
    A. keep a copy of heart attack procedures on file so that it can be referenced to by any member of the staff when an emergency occurs
    B. provide each member of the staff with a first aid book which is to be kept in an accessible location
    C. train all members of the staff in the proper procedure for handling such emergencies, assigning specific responsibilities
    D. post, in several places around the office, a list of specific procedures to follow in each of several different emergencies

18._____

19. Your superior has subscribed to several publications directly related to your divisions work, and he has asked you to see to it that the publications are circulated among the supervisory personnel in the division. There are eight supervisors involved.
The BEST method of insuring that all eight see these publications is to
    A. place the publication in the division's general reference library as soon as it arrives
    B. inform each supervisor whenever a publication arrives and remind all of them that they are responsible for reading it
    C. prepare a standard slip that can be stapled to each publication, listing the eight supervisors and saying, *Please read, initial your name, and pass along*
    D. send a memo to the eight supervisors saying that they may wish to purchase individual subscriptions in their own names if they are interested in seeing each issue

19._____

20. Assume that you have been asked to prepare a narrative summary of the monthly reports submitted by employees in your division.
In preparing your summary of this month's reports, the FIRST step to take is to
    A. read through the reports, noting their general content and any unusual features
    B. decide how many typewritten pages your summary should contain

20._____

C. make a written summary of each separate report, so that you will not have to go back to the original reports again
D. ask each employee which points he would prefer to see emphasized in your summary

21. Your superior has telephoned a number of key officials in your agency to ask whether they can meet at a certain time next month. He has found that they can all make it, and he has asked you to confirm the meeting.
Which of the following is the BEST way to confirm such a meeting?
    A. Note the meeting on your superior's calendar
    B. Post a notice of the meeting on the agency bulletin board
    C. Call the officials on the day of the meeting to remind them of the meeting
    D. Write a memo to each official involved repeating the time and place of the meeting

21.____

22. Of the following, the worker who is MOST likely to create a problem in maintaining safety is one who
    A. disregards hazards   B. feels tired
    C. resents authority   D. gets bored

22.____

23. Assume that a new regulation requires that certain kinds of private organizations file information forms with your department. You have been asked to write the short explanatory message that will be printed on the front cover of the pamphlet containing the forms and instructions.
Which of the following would be the MOST appropriate way of beginning this message?
    A. Get the readers' attention by emphasizing immediately that there are legal penalties for organizations that fail to file before a certain date
    B. Briefly state the nature of the enclosed forms and the types of organizations that must file
    C. Say that your department is very sorry to have to put organizations to such an inconvenience
    D. Quote the entire regulation adopted by the city, even if it is quite long and is expressed in complicated legal language

23.____

24. Suppose that you have been told to make up the vacation schedule for the 15 employees in a particular unit. In order for the unit to operate effectively, only a few employees can be on vacation at the same time.
Which of the following is the MOST advisable approach in making up the schedule?
    A. Draw up a schedule assigning vacations in alphabetical order
    B. Find out when the supervisors want to take their vacations, and randomly assign whatever periods are left to the non-supervisory personnel
    C. Assign the most desirable times to employees of longest standing, and the least desirable times to the newest employees
    D. Have all employees state their own preferences, and then work out any conflicts in consultation with the people involved

24.____

25. Assume that you have been asked to prepare job descriptions for various positions in your department.
Which of the following are the BASIC points that should be covered in a job description?
   A. General duties and responsibilities of the position, with examples of day-to-day tasks
   B. Comments on the performances of present employees
   C. Estimates of the number of openings that may be available in each category during the coming year
   D. Instructions for carrying out the specific tasks assigned to your department

25._____

KEY (CORRECT ANSWERS)

1.	A	11.	A
2.	C	12.	B
3.	B	13.	A
4.	B	14.	A
5.	A	15.	A
6.	D	16.	A
7.	A	17.	D
8.	D	18.	C
9.	B	19.	C
10.	D	20.	A

21.	D
22.	A
23.	B
24.	D
25.	A

TEST 3

DIRECTIONS: Each question or incomplete statement is followed by several suggested answers or completions. Select the one that BEST answers the question or completes the statement. *PRINT THE LETTER OF THE CORRECT ANSWER IN THE SPACE AT THE RIGHT.*

Questions 1-6.

DIRECTIONS: Questions 1 through 6 consist of sets of names and addresses. In each question, the name and address in Column II should be an exact copy of the name and address in Column I. If there is:
a mistake only in the name, mark your answer A;
a mistake only in the address, mark your answer B;
a mistake in both name and address, mark your answer C;
NO mistake in either name or address, mark your answer D.

SAMPLE QUESTION

COLUMN I
Christina Magnusson
288 Greene Street
New York, NY 10003

COLUMN II
Christina Magnusson
288 Greene Street
New York, NY 10013

Since there is a mistake only in the address (the zone number should be 10003 instead of 10013), the answer to the sample question is B.

COLUMN I   COLUMN II

1. Ms. Joan Kelly   Ms. Joan Kielly   1.____
    313 Franklin Ave.   318 Franklin Ave.
    Brooklyn, NY 11202   Brooklyn, NY 11202

2. Mrs. Eileen Engel   Mrs. Ellen Engel   2.____
    47-24 86 Road   47-24 86 Road
    Queens, NY 11122   Queens, NY 11122

3. Marcia Michaels   Marcia Michaels   3.____
    213 E. 81 St.   213 E. 81 St.
    New York, NY 10012   New York, NY 10012

4. Rev. Edward J. Smyth   Rev. Edward J. Smyth   4.____
    1401 Brandeis Street   1401 Brandies Street
    San Francisco, CA 96201   San Francisco, CA 96201

5. Alicia Rodriguez   Alicia Rodriguez   5.____
    24-68 81 St.   2468 81 St.
    Elmhurst, NY 11122   Elmhurst, NY 11122

2 (#3)

COLUMN I	COLUMN II	
6. Ernest Eisemann 21 Columbia St. New York, NY 10007	Ernest Eisermann 21 Columbia St. New York, NY 10007	6.____

Questions 7-11.

DIRECTIONS: Questions 7 through 11 each consist of five serial numbers which must be arranged according to the directions given below.

The serial numbers of dollar bills in Column I begin and end with a capital letter and have an eight-digit number in between. They are to be arranged as follows:

First: In alphabetical order according to the first letter.
Second: When two or more serial numbers have the same first letter, in alphabetical order according to the last letter.
Third: When two or more serial numbers have the same first and last letters, in numerical order, beginning with the lowest number.

The serial numbers in Column I are numbered (1) through (5) in the order in which they are listed. In Column II, the numbers (1) through (5) are arranged in four different ways to show different arrangements of the corresponding serial numbers. Choose the answer in Column II in which the serial numbers are arranged according to the above rules.
SAMPLE QUESTION:

	COLUMN I		COLUMN II
(1)	E75044127B	(A)	4, 1, 3, 2, 5
(2)	B96399104A	(B)	4, 1 2, 3, 5
(3)	B93939086A	(C)	4, 3, 2 5, 1
(4)	B47064465H	(D)	3, 2, 5, 4, 1
(5)	B99040922A		

In the sample question, the four serial numbers starting with B should be put before the serial numbers starting with E. The serial numbers starting with B and ending with A should be put before the serial number starting with B and ending with H. The three serial numbers starting with B and ending with A should be listed in numerical order, beginning with the lowest number. The correct way to arrange the serial numbers, therefore, is

(3) B93939086A
(2) B96399104A
(5) B99040922A
(4) B47064465H
(1) B75044127B

Since the order of arrangement is 3, 2, 5, 4, 1, the answer to the sample question is (D).

53

3 (#3)

	COLUMN I	COLUMN II	
7.	(1) S55126179E (2) R55136177Q (3) P55126177R (4) S55126178R (5) R55126180P	A. 1, 5, 2, 3, 4 B. 3, 4, 1, 5, 2 C. 3, 5, 2, 1, 4 D. 4, 3, 1, 5, 2	7.____
8.	(1) T64217813Q (2) I64217817O (3) T64218180 (4) I64217811Q (5) T64217816Q	A. 4, 1, 3, 2, 5 B. 2, 4, 3, 1, 5 C. 4, 1, 5, 2, 3 D. 2, 3, 4, 1, 5	8.____
9.	(1) C83261824G (2) C78361833C (3) G83261732G (4) C88261823C (5) G83261743C	A. 2, 4, 1, 5, 3 B. 4, 2, 1, 3, 5 C. 3, 1, 5, 2, 4 D. 2, 3, 5, 1, 4	9.____
10.	(1) A11710107H (2) H17110017A (3) A11170707A (4) II17170171H (5) A11710177A	A. 2, 1, 4, 3, 5 B. 3, 1, 5, 2, 4 C. 3, 4, 1, 5, 2 D. 3, 5, 1, 2, 4	10.____
11.	(1) R26794821S (2) O26794821T (3) M26794827Z (4) Q26794821R (5) S26794821P	A. 3, 2, 4, 1, 5 B. 3, 4, 2, 1, 5 C. 4, 2, 1, 3, 5 D. 5, 4, 1, 2, 3	11.____

Questions 12-16.

DIRECTIONS: Questions 12 through 16 each consist of three lines of code letters and numbers. The numbers on each line should correspond with the code letters on the same line in accordance with the table below.

Code Letters	Q	S	L	Y	M	O	U	N	W	Z
Corresponding Numbers	1	2	3	4	5	6	7	8	9	0

On some of the lines, an error exists in the coding. Compare the letters and numbers in each question carefully. If you find an error on:
   only ONE of the lines in the question, mark your answer A;
   any TWO lines in the question, mark your answer B;
   all THREE lines in the question, mark your answer C;
   NONE of the lines in the question, mark your answer D.

SAMPLE: MOQNWZQS – 56189012
            QWNMOLYU – 19865347
            LONLMYWN – 36835489

In the above sample, the first line is correct since each code letter, as listed, has the correct corresponding number. On the second line, an error exists because code letter M should have the letter number 5 instead of the number 6. On the third line, an error exists because the code letter W should have the number 9 instead of the number 8. Since there are errors on two of the three lines, the correct answer is B.

12.	SMUWOLQN	25796318	12.____
	ULSQNMZL	73218503	
	NMYQZUSL	85410723	
13.	YUWWMYQZ	47995410	13.____
	SOSOSQSO	26262126	
	ZUNLWMYW	07839549	
14.	QULSWZYN	17329045	14.____
	ZYLQWOYW	04319639	
	QLUYWZSO	13749026	
15.	NLQZOYUM	83106475	15.____
	SQMUWZOM	21579065	
	MMYWMZSQ	55498021	
16.	NQLOWZZU	81319007	16.____
	SMYLUNZO	25347806	
	UWMSNZOL	79528013	

Questions 17-24.

DIRECTIONS: Each of Questions 17 through 24 represents five cards to be filed, numbered 1 through 5 in Column I. Each card is made up of the employee's name, the date of a work assignment, and the work assignment code number shown in parentheses. The cards are to be filed according to the following rules.

First: File in alphabetical order.
Second: When two or more cards have the same employee's name, file according to the assignment date beginning with the earliest date.
Third: When to or more cards have the same employee's name and the same date, file according to the work assignment number beginning with the lowest number.

Column II shows the cards arranged in four different orders. Pick the answer (A, B, C, or D) in Column which shows the cards arranged correctly according to the above filing rules.

17. B
18. A
19. B
20. D

6 (#3)

21.	(1)	Eger	4/19/19	(874129)	A. 3, 4, 1, 2, 5	21.____
	(2)	Eihler	5/19/20	(875329)	B. 1, 4, 5, 2, 3	
	(3)	Ehrlich	11/19/19	(874839)	C. 4, 1, 3, 2, 5	
	(4)	Eger	4/19/19	(876129)	D. 1, 4, 3, 5, 2	
	(5)	Eihler	5/19/19	(874239)		
22.	(1)	Johnson	12/21/19	(786814)	A. 2, 4, 3, 5, 1	22.____
	(2)	Johns	12/21/20	(801024)	B. 4, 2, 5, 3, 1	
	(3)	Johnson	12/12/20	(762814)	C. 4, 5, 3, 1, 2	
	(4)	Jackson	12/12/20	(862934)	D. 5, 3, 1, 2, 4	
	(5)	Johnson	12/12/20	(762184)		
23.	(1)	Fuller	7/12/19	(598310)	A. 2, 1, 5, 4, 3	23.____
	(2)	Fuller	7/2/19	(598301)	B. 1, 2, 4, 5, 3	
	(3)	Fuller	7/22/19	(598410)	C. 1, 4, 5, 2, 3	
	(4)	Fuller	7/17/20	(598710)	D. 2, 1, 3, 5, 3	
	(5)	Fuller	7/17/20	(598701)		
24.	(1)	Perrine	10/27/16	(637096)	A. 3, 4, 5, 1, 2	24.____
	(2)	Perrone	11/14/19	(767609)	B. 3, 2, 5, 4, 1	
	(3)	Perrault	10/15/15	(629706)	C. 5, 3, 1, 4, 2	
	(4)	Perrine	10/17/19	(373656)	D. 4, 5, 1, 2, 3	
	(5)	Perine	10/17/18	(376356)		

Questions 25-30.

DIRECTIONS: Questions 25 through 30 are to be answered on the basis of the information given in the following passage.

It is often said that no system will work if the people who carry it out do not want it to work. In too many cases, a departmental reorganization that seemed technically sound and economically practical has proved to be a failure because the planners neglected to take the human factor into account. The truth is that employees are likely to feel threatened when they learn that a major change is in the wind. It does not matter whether or not the change actually poses a threat to an employee; the fact that he believes it does or fears it might is enough to make him feel insecure. Among the dangers he fears, the foremost is the possibility that his job may cease to exist and that he may be laid off or shunted into a less skilled position at lower pay. Even if he knows that his own job category is secure, however, he is likely to fear losing some of the important intangible advantages of his present position for instance, he may fear that he will be separated from his present companions and thrust in with a group of strangers, or that he will find himself in a lower position on the organizational ladder if a new position is created above his.

It is important that management recognize these natural fears and take them into account in planning any kind of major change. While there is no cut-and-dried formula for preventing employee resistance, there are several steps that can be taken to reduce employees' fears and gain their cooperation. First, unwarranted fears can be dispelled if employees are kept informed of the planning from the start and if they know exactly what to expect. Next, assurance on matters such as retraining, transfers, and placement help should be given as soon as it is clear what direction the reorganization will take. Finally, employees' participation in the planning should be actively sought. There is a great psychological difference between feeling that a change is being forced upon one from the outside, and feeling that one is an insider who is helping to bring about a change.

25. According to the above passage, employees who are not in real danger of losing their jobs because of a proposed reorganization
    A. will be eager to assist in the reorganization
    B. will pay little attention to the reorganization
    C. should not be taken into account in planning the reorganization
    D. are nonetheless likely to feel threatened by the reorganization

26. The above passage mentions the *intangible advantages* of a position. Which of the following BEST describes the kind of advantages alluded to in the passage?
    A. Benefits such as paid holidays and vacations
    B. Satisfaction of human needs for things like friendship and status
    C. Qualities such as leadership and responsibility
    D. A work environment that meets satisfactory standards of health and safety

27. According to the above passage, an employee's fear that a reorganization may separate him from his present companions is a(n)
    A. childish and immature reaction to change
    B. unrealistic feeling, since this is not going to happen
    C. possible reaction that the planners should be aware of
    D. incentive to employees to participate in the planning

28. On the basis of the above passage, it would be *desirable*, when planning a departmental reorganization, to
    A. be governed by employee feelings and attitudes
    B. give some employees lower positions
    C. keep employees informed
    D. lay off those who are less skilled

29. What does the above passage say can be done to help gain employees' cooperation in a reorganization?
    A. Making sure that the change is technically sound, that it is economically practical, and that the human factor is taken into account
    B. Keeping employees fully informed, offering help in fitting them into new positions, and seeking their participation in the planning
    C. Assuring employees that they will not be laid off, that they will not be reassigned to a group of strangers, and that no new positions will be created on the organization ladder
    D. Reducing employees' fears, arranging a retraining program, and providing for transfers

30. Which of the following suggested title would be MOST appropriate for this passage? 30._____
    A. Planning a Departmental Reorganization
    B. Why Employees are Afraid
    C. Looking Ahead to the Future
    D. Planning for Change: The Human Factor

KEY (CORRECT ANSWERS)

1.	C	11.	A	21.	D
2.	A	12.	D	22.	B
3.	D	13.	D	23.	D
4.	B	14.	B	24.	C
5.	C	15.	A	25.	D
6.	A	16.	C	26.	B
7.	C	17.	B	27.	C
8.	B	18.	A	28.	C
9.	A	19.	B	29.	B
10.	D	20.	D	30.	D

EXAMINATION SECTION

TEST 1

DIRECTIONS: Each question or incomplete statement is followed by several suggested answers or completions. Select the one that BEST answers the question or completes the statement. *PRINT THE LETTER OF THE CORRECT ANSWER IN THE SPACE AT THE RIGHT.*

Questions 1-6.

DIRECTIONS: Questions 1 through 6 are to be answered SOLELY on the basis of the numbered boxes on the Arrest Report and paragraph below.

ARREST REPORT

1. Arrest Number	2. Precinct of Arrest		3. Date/Time of Arrest	4. Defendant's Name	5. Defendant's Address
6. Defendant's Date of Birth	7. Sex	8. Race	9. Height	10. Weight	11. Location of Arrest	12. Date and Time of Occurrence
13. Location of Occurrence	14. Complaint Number		15. Victim's Name	16. Victim's Address	17. Victim's Date of Birth
18. Precinct of Complaint	19. Arresting Officer's Name		20. Shield Number	21. Assigned Unit Precinct	2. Date of Complaint

On Friday, December 13 at 11:45 P.M., while leaving a store at 235 Spring Street, Grace O'Connell, a white female, 5'2" 130 lbs., was approached by a white male, 5'11", 200 lbs., who demanded her money and jewelry. As the man ran and turned down River Street, Police Officer William James, Shield Number 31724, assigned to the 14th Precinct, gave chase and apprehended him in front of 523 River Street. The prisoner, Gerald Grande, who resides at 17 Water Street, was arrested at 12:05 A.M., was charged with robbery, and taken to the 13th Precinct, where he was assigned Arrest Number 53048. Miss O'Connell, who resides at 275 Spring St., was given Complaint Number 822460.

1. On the basis of the Arrest Report and the above paragraph, the CORRECT entry for Box Number 3 should be
   A. 11:45 P.M., 12/13
   B. 11:45 P.M., 12/14
   C. 12:05 A.M., 12/13
   D. 12:05 A.M., 12/14

    1.____

2. On the basis of the Arrest Report and the above paragraph, the CORRECT entry for Box Number 21 should be
   A. 12th Precinct
   B. 14th Precinct
   C. Mounted Unit
   D. 32nd Precinct

    2.____

3. On the basis of the Arrest Report and the above paragraph, the CORRECT entry for Box Number 11 should be
   A. 235 Spring St.
   B. 523 River St.
   C. 275 Spring St.
   D. 17 Water St.

3.____

4. On the basis of the Arrest Report and the above paragraph, the CORRECT entry for Box Number 2 should be
   A. 13th Precinct
   B. 14th Precinct
   C. Mounted Unit
   D. 32nd Precinct

4.____

5. On the basis of the Arrest Report and the above paragraph, the CORRECT entry for Box Number 13 should be
   A. 523 River St.
   B. 17 Water St.
   C. 275 Spring St.
   D. 235 Spring St.

5.____

6. On the basis of the Arrest Report and the above paragraph, the CORRECT entry for Box Number 14 should be
   A. 53048
   B. 31724
   C. 12/13
   D. 82460

6.____

Questions 7-10.

DIRECTIONS: Questions 7 through 10 are to be answered SOLELY on the basis of the following information.

You are required to file various documents in file drawers which are labeled according to the following pattern:

DOCUMENTS

MEMOS		LETTERS		REPORTS		INQUIRIES	
File	Subject	File	Subject	File	Subject	File	Subject
84PM1	(A-L)	84PC1	(A-L)	84PR1	(A-L)	84PQ1	(A-L)
84PM2	(M-Z)	84PC2	(M-Z)	84PR2	(M-Z)	84PQ2	(M-Z)

7. A letter dealing with a burglary should be filed in the drawer labeled
   A. 84PM1   B. 84PC1   C. 84PR1   D. 84PQ2

7.____

8. A report on *Statistics* should be found in the drawer labeled
   A. 84PM1   B. 84PC2   C. 84PR2   D. 84PQ2

8.____

9. An inquiry is received about parade permit procedures. It should be filed in the drawer labeled
   A. 84PM2   B. 84PC1   C. 84PR1   D. 84PQ2

9.____

10. A police officer has a question about a robbery report you filed. You should pull this file from the drawer labeled
    A. 84PM1   B. 84PM2   C. 84PR1   D. 84PR2

10.____

Questions 11-18.

DIRECTIONS: Questions 11 through 18 are to be answered SOLELY on the basis of the following information.

Below are listed the code number, name, and area of investigation of six detective units. Each question describes a crime.

For each question, choose the option (A, B, C, or D) which contains the code number for the detective unit responsible for handling that crime.

DETECTIVE UNITS

Unit Code No.	Unit Name	Unit's Area of Investigation
01	Senior Citizens Unit	All robberies of senior citizens 65 years or older
02	Major Case Unit	Any bank robbery; a commercial robbery where value of goods or money stolen is over $25,000
03	Robbery Unit	Any commercial, non-bank robbery where the value of the stolen goods or money is $25,000 or less; robberies of individuals under 65 years of age
04	Fraud and Larceny Unit	Confidence games and pickpockets
05	Special Investigations Unit	Burglaries of premises where the value of goods removed or monies taken is $15,000 or less
06	Burglary Unit	Burglaries of premises where the value of goods removed or monies taken is over $15,000

11. Mrs. Green calls the precinct and reports that her apartment was burglarized while she was on vacation and that precious jewelry and silverware, valued at $27,000, were taken.
    To which unit code number should her complaint be referred?
    A. 05   B. 02   C. 03   D. 06

12. Sylvia Bailey, Manager of the Building and Loan Savings Bank, reports that a man handed one of her tellers a note stating, *This is a robbery*. He had a gun and demanded money. The teller gave the man $500 in small bills, and the man then left.
    To which unit code should the complaint be referred?
    A. 02   B. 06   C. 03   D. 05

13. Mrs. Miniver, a 67-year-old widow, states that she was beaten and robbed by two men in the elevator of her apartment building.
    To which unit code number should the complaint be referred?
    A. 06   B. 01   C. 03   D. 02

13._____

14. Mr. Whipple, Manager of T.V.A. Supermarket, reports that during the night someone entered the store and removed merchandise valued at $12,500.
    To which unit code number should the complaint be referred?
    A. 05   B. 03   C. 06   D. 02

14._____

15. Mr. Gold, owner of Gold's Jewelry Exchange, reports that two men, armed with shotguns, robbed his store and removed money and jewelry valued at $28,000.
    To which unit code number should the complaint be referred?
    A. 05   B. 03   C. 06   D. 02

15._____

16. Mr. Watson, a 62-year-old man, was walking in Central Park when he was approached by a man with a knife and was robbed of $72.
    To which unit code number should the complaint be referred?
    A. 01   B. 06   C. 03   D. 02

16._____

17. The Ace Jewelry Manufacturing Company was broken into over the weekend when the building was closed. The owner stated that $35,000 in gold, silver, diamonds, and jewelry were taken.
    To which unit code number should the complaint be referred?
    A. 02   B. 03   C. 06   D. 05

17._____

18. Mrs. Vargas, 62, reports that she gave Mr. Greene of the Starlite Realty Corporation $1,000 to locate a new apartment for her family. A week went by, and she never heard from Mr. Greene. She called the Starlite Realty Corporation, and they informed her that Mr. Greene never worked for Starlite Realty Corporation and that they have no record of the $1,000 deposit of Mrs. Vargas.
    To which unit code number should the complaint be referred?
    A. 04   B. 03   C. 01   D. 05

18._____

Questions 19-24.

DIRECTIONS: Questions 19 through 24 consist of sentences which contain examples of correct or incorrect English usage. Examine each sentence with reference to grammar, spelling, punctuation, and capitalization. Choose one of the following options that would be BEST for correct English usage:
  A. The sentence is correct.
  B. There is one mistake.
  C. There are two mistakes.
  D. There are three mistakes.

19. Mrs. Fitzgerald came to the 59th Precinct to retreive her property which were stolen earlier in the week.

19._____

5 (#1)

20. The two officer's responded to the call, only to find that the perpatrator and the 20._____
victim have left the scene.

21. Mr. Coleman called the 61st Precinct to report that, upon arriving at his store, 21._____
he discovered that there was a large hole in the wall and that three boxes of
radios were missing

22. The Administrative Leiutenant of the 62nd Precinct held a meeting which was 22._____
attended by all the civilians, assigned to the Precinct.

23. Three days after the robbery occured the detective apprahended two 23._____
suspects and recovered the stolen items.

24. The Community Affairs Officer of the 64th Precinct is the liaison between 24._____
the Precinct and the community; he works closely with various community
organizations, and elected officials.

Questions 25-32.

DIRECTIONS: Questions 25 through 32 are to be answered on the basis of the following
paragraph, which contains some deliberate errors in spelling and/or grammar
and/or punctuation. Each line of the paragraph is preceded by a number.
There are 9 lines and 9 numbers.

Line No.	Paragraph Line
1	The protection of life and property are, one of
2	the oldest and most important functions of a city.
3	New York city has its own full-time police Agency.
4	The police Department has the power an it shall
5	be there duty to preserve the Public piece,
6	prevent crime detect and arrest offenders, suppress
7	riots, protect the rites of persons and property, etc.
8	The maintainance of sound relations with the community they
9	serve is an important function of law enforcement officers.

25. How many errors are contained in line one? 25._____
   A. One   B. Two   C. Three   D. None

26. How many errors are contained in line two? 26._____
   A. One   B. Two   C. Three   D. None

27. How many errors are contained in line three? 27._____
   A. One   B. Two   C. Three   D. None

28. How many errors are contained in line four? 28._____
   A. One   B. Two   C. Three   D. None

29. How many errors are contained in line five?
    A. One   B. Two   C. Three   D. None   29._____

30. How many errors are contained in line six?
    A. One   B. Two   C. Three   D. None   30._____

31. How many errors are contained in line seven?
    A. One   B. Two   C. Three   D. None   31._____

32. How many errors are contained in line eight?
    A. One   B. Two   C. Three   D. None   32._____

Questions 33-40.

DIRECTIONS: Questions 33 through 40 are to be answered on the basis of the material contained in the INDEX OF CRIME IN CENTRAL CITY, U.S.A. 2011-2020 appearing below. Certain information is various columns is deliberately left blank.
The correct answer (A, B, C, or D) to these questions requires you to make computations that will enable you to fill in the blanks correctly.

INDEX OF CRIME IN CENTRAL CITY, U.S.A., 2011-2020									
	Crime Index Total	Violent Crime[1]	Property Crime[2]	Murder	Forcible Rape	Robbery	Aggravated Assault	Burglary	Larceny Theft	Motor Vehicle Theft
2011	8,717	875		19	51	385	420	2,565	4,347	930
2012	10,252	974	9278	20	55	443	456		5,262	977
2013	11,256	1,026	10,230	20		465	485	3,253	5,977	1,000
2014	11,304	986		18	58	420	490	3,089	6,270	959
2015	10,935	1,009	9,926	19	63	405	522	3,053	5,605	968
2016	11,140	1,061	10,079	19	67	417	558	3,104	5,983	992
2017	12,152	1,178	10,974	23	75	466	614	3,299	6,578	1,097
2018	13,294	1,308	11,986	23	83		654	3,759	7,113	1,114
2019	13,289	1,321	11,968	22	82	574	643	3,740	7,154	1,074
2020	12,856	1,285	11,571	22	77	536	650	3,415	7,108	1,048

33. What was the TOTAL number of Property Crimes in 2011?   33._____
    A. 9,740   B. 10,252   C. 16,559   D. 7,842

34. What was the TOTAL number of Burglaries for 2012?   34._____
    A. 2,062   B. 3,039   C. 3,259   D. 4,001

35. In 2020, the total number of Aggravated Assaults was MOST NEARLY what 35._____
    percent of the total number of Violent Crimes for that year?
    A. 49.1   B. 46.3   C. 50.6   D. 41.7

36. In 2015, Property Crime was MOST NEARLY what percent of the Crime   36._____
    Index Total?
    A. 90.8   B. 9.3   C. 10.1   D. 89.9

37. What was the TOTAL number of Property Crimes for 2014? 37.____
    A. 10,318   B. 11,304   C. 98   D. 10,808

38. What was the TOTAL number of Robberies for 2018? 38.____
    A. 654   B. 571   C. 548   D. 1,202

39. Robbery made up what percent of the TOTAL number of Violent Crimes for 2020? 39.____
    A. 68.8%   B. 4.1%   C. 21.9%   D. 41.7%

40. What was the TOTAL number of Forcible Rapes for 2013? 40.____
    A. 47   B. 56   C. 55   D. 101

KEY (CORRECT ANSWERS)

1.	D	11.	D	21.	A	31.	A
2.	B	12.	A	22.	C	32.	A
3.	B	13.	B	23.	C	33.	D
4.	A	14.	A	24.	B	34.	B
5.	D	15.	D	25.	C	35.	C
6.	D	16.	C	26.	D	36.	A
7.	B	17.	C	27.	C	37.	A
8.	C	18.	A	28.	B	38.	C
9.	D	19.	C	29.	C	39.	D
10.	D	20.	D	30.	B	40.	B

TEST 2

DIRECTIONS: Each question or incomplete statement is followed by several suggested answers or completions. Select the one that BEST answers the question or completes the statement. *PRINT THE LETTER OF THE CORRECT ANSWER IN THE SPACE AT THE RIGHT.*

Questions 1-8.

DIRECTIONS: Each of Questions 1 through 8 consists of three lines of code letters and numbers. The numbers on each line should correspond to the code letters on the same line in accordance with the table below.

Code Letter	X	B	L	T	V	M	P	F	J	S
Corresponding Number	0	1	2	3	4	5	6	7	8	9

On some of the lines, an error exists in the coding. Compare the letters and numbers in each question carefully. If you find an error or errors on:
Only <u>one</u> of the lines in the question, mark your answer A;
Any <u>two</u> of the lines in the question, mark your answer B;
All <u>three</u> lines in the question, mark your answer C;
<u>None</u> of the lines in the question, mark your answer D.

<u>SAMPLE QUESTION</u>: MSXVLPT—5904263
SBFJLTP—9178246
XVMBTPF—8451367

In the above sample, the first line is correct since each code letter listed has the correct corresponding number. On the second line, an error exists because code letter T should have number 3 instead of number 4. On the third line, an error exists because the code letter X should have the number 0 instead of the number 8. Since there are errors on two of the three lines, the correct answer is B.

1. VFSTPLM—4793625
    SBXFLTP—9017236
    BT[JFSV—1358794

1.____

2. TSLFVPJ—3927468
    JLFTVXS—8273409
    MVSXBFL—5490172

2.____

3. XFTJSVT—0739843
    VFMTFLB—4753721
    LTFJSFM—2378985

3.____

4. SJMSJVL—9859742
    VFBXMPF—3710568
    PFPXLBS—7670219

4.____

2 (#2)

5. MFPXVFP—5764076
   PTFJBLX—6378120
   VXSVSTB—4094931

5.____

6. BXFPVJT—1076483
   STFMVLT—9375423
   TXPBTTM—3061335

6.____

7. VLSBLVP—4290246
   FPSFBMV—7679154
   XTMXMLL—0730522

7.____

8. JFVPMTJ—8746538
   TFPMXBL—3765012
   TJSFMFX—4987570

8.____

Questions 9-18.

DIRECTIONS: Questions 9 through 18 each consists of two columns, each containing four lines of names, numbers and/or addresses. For each question, compare the lines in Column I with the lines in Column II to see if they match exactly, and mark your answer (A, B, C, or D) according to the following instructions:
- A. all four lines match exactly
- B. only three lines match exactly
- C. only two lines match exactly
- D. only one line matches exactly

9. (1) Earl Hodgson   Earl Hodgson
   (2) 1409870   1408970
   (3) Shore Ave.   Schore Ave.
   (4) Macon Rd.   Macon Rd.

9.____

10. (1) 9671485   9671485
    (2) 470 Astor Court   470 Astor Court
    (3) Halprin, Phillip   Halperin, Phillip
    (4) Frank D. Poliseo   Frank D. Poliseo

10.____

11. (1) Tandem Associates   Tandom Associates
    (2) 144-17 Northern Blvd.   144-17 Northern Blvd.
    (3) Alberta Forchi   Albert Forchi
    (4) Kings Park, NY 10751   Kings Point, NY 10751

11.____

12. (1) Bertha C. McCormack   Bertha C. McCormack
    (2) Clayton, MO   Clayton, MO
    (3) 976-4242   976-4242
    (4) New City, NY 10951   New City, NY 10951

12.____

69

13. (1) George C. Morill   George C. Morrill   13.____
    (2) Columbia, SC 29201   Columbia, SD 29201
    (3) Louis Ingham   Louis Ingham
    (4) 3406 Forest Ave.   3406 Forest Ave.

14. (1) 506 S. Elliott Pl.   506 S. Elliott Pl.   14.____
    (2) Herbert Hall   Hurbert Hall
    (3) 4712 Rockaway Pkway   4712 Rockaway Pkway
    (4) 169 E. 7 St.   169 E. 7 St.

15. (1) 345 Park Ave.   345 Park Pl.   15.____
    (2) Colman Oven Corp.   Coleman Oven Corp.
    (3) Robert Conte   Robert Conti
    (4) 6179846   6179846

16. (1) Grigori Schierber   Grigori Schierber   16.____
    (2) Des Moines, Iowa   Des Moines, Iowa
    (3) Gouverneur Hospital   Gouverneur Hospital
    (4) 91-35 Cresskill Pl.   91-35 Cresskill Pl.

17. (1) Jeffery Janssen   Jeffrey Janssen   17.____
    (2) 8041071   8041071
    (3) 40 Rockefeller Plaza   40 Rockafeller Plaza
    (4) 407 6 St.   406 7 St.

18. (1) 5971996   5871996   18.____
    (2) 3113 Knickerbocker Ave.   3113 Knickerbocker Ave.
    (3) 8434 Boston Post Rd.   8424 Boston Post Rd.
    (4) Penn Station   Penn Station

Questions 19-22.

DIRECTIONS: Questions 19 through 22 are to be answered by looking at the 4 groups of names and addresses listed below (I, II, III, and IV) and then finding out the number of groups that have their corresponding numbered lines exactly the same.

Group I
Line 1 Ingersoll Public Library
Line 2 Reference and Research Dept.
Line 3 95-12 238 St.
Line 4 East Elmhurst, N.Y. 11357

Group II
Ingersoil Public Library
Reference and Research Dept.
95-12 238 St.
East Elmhurst, N.Y. 11357

Group III
Line 1 Ingersoll Public Library
Line 2 Reference and Research Dept.
Line 3 92-15 283 St.
Line 4 East Elmhurst, N.Y. 11357

Group IV
Ingersoll Poblic Library
Referance and Research Dept.
95-12 283 St.
East Elmhurst, N.Y. 1357

19. In how many groups is line one exactly the same? 19._____
    A. Two   B. Three   C. Four   D. None

20. In how many groups is line two exactly the same? 20._____
    A. Two   B. Three   C. Four   D. None

21. In how many groups is line three exactly the same? 20._____
    A. Two   B. Three   C. Four   D. None

22. In how many groups is line four exactly the same? 22._____
    A. Two   B. Three   C. Four   E. None

Questions 23-26.

DIRECTIONS: Questions 23 through 26 are to be answered by looking at the 4 groups of names and addresses listed below (I, II, III, and IV) and then finding out the number of groups that have their corresponding numbered lines exactly the same.

Group I
Line 1 Richmond General Hospital
Line 2 Geriatric Clinic
Line 3 3975 Paerdegat St.
Line 4 Loudonville, New York 11538

Group II
Richman General Hospital
Geriatric Clinic
3975 Peardegat St.
Londonville, New York 11538

Group III
Line 1 Richmond General Hospital
Line 2 Geriatric Clinic
Line 3 3795 Paerdegat St.
Line 4 Loudonville, New York 11358

Group IV
Richmend General Hospital
Geriatric Clinic
3975 Paerdegat St.
Loudonville, New York 11538

23. In how many groups is line one exactly the same? 23._____
    A. Two   B. Three   C. Four   D. None

24. In how many groups is line two exactly the same? 24._____
    A. Two   B. Three   C. Four   D. None

25. In how many groups is line three exactly the same? 25._____
    A. Two   B. Three   C. Four   D. None

26. In how many groups is line four exactly the same? 26._____
    A. Two   B. Three   C. Four   D. None

Questions 27-34.

DIRECTIONS: Each of Questions 27 through 34 consists of four or six numbered names. For each question, choose the option (A, B, C, or D) which indicates the order in which the names should be filed in accordance with the following file instructions:

5 (#2)

- File alphabetically according to last name, then first name, then middle initial.
- File according to each successive letter within a name.
- When comparing two names where the letters in the longer name are identical with the corresponding letters in the shorter name, the shorter name is filed first.
- When the last names are the same, initials are always filed before names beginning with the same letter.

27. I. Ralph Robinson
    II. Alfred Ross
    III. Luis Robles
    IV. James Roberts
    The CORRECT filing sequence for the above names should be
    A. IV, II, I, III   B. I, IV, III, II   C. III, IV, I, II   D. IV, I, III, II

28. I. Irwin Goodwin
    II. Inez Gonzalez
    III. Irene Goodman
    IV. Ira S. Goodwin
    V. Ruth I. Goldstein
    VI. M.B. Goodman
    The CORRECT filing sequence for the above names should be
    A. V, II, I, IV, III, VI
    B. V, II, VI, III, IV, I
    C. V, II, III, VI, IV, I
    D. V, II, III, VI, I, IV

29. I. George Allan
    II. Gregory Allen
    III. Gary Allen
    IV. George Allen
    The CORRECT filing sequence for the above names should be
    A. IV, III, I, II   B. I, IV, II, III   C. III, IV, I, II   D. I, III, IV, II

30. I. Simon Kauffman
    II. Leo Kauffman
    III. Robert Kaufmann
    IV. Paul Kauffman
    The CORRECT filing sequence for the above names should be
    A. I, IV, II, III   B. II, IV, I, III   C. III, II, IV, I   D. I, II, III, IV

31. I. Roberta Williams
    II. Robin Wilson
    III. Roberta Wilson
    IV. Robin Williams
    The CORRECT filing sequence for the above names should be
    A. III, II, IV, I   B. I, IV, III, II   C. I, II, III, IV   D. III, I, II, IV

32. I. Lawrence Shultz
     II. Albert Schultz
     III. Theodore Schwartz
     IV. Thomas Schwarz
     V. Alvin Schultz
     VI. Leonard Shultz
     The CORRECT filing sequence for the above names should be
     A. II, V, III, IV, I, VI   B. IV, III, V, I, II, VI
     C. II, V, I, VI, III, IV   D. I, VI, II, V, III, IV

33. I. McArdle
     II. Mayer
     III. Maletz
     IV. McNiff
     V. Meyer
     VI. MacMahon
     The CORRECT filing sequence for the above names should be
     A. I, IV, VI, III, II, V   B. II, I, IV, VI, III, V
     C. VI, III, II, I, IV, V   D. VI, III, II, V, I, IV

34. I. Jack E. Johnson
     II. R.H. Jackson
     III. Bertha Jackson
     IV. J.T. Johnson
     V. Ann Johns
     VI. John Jacobs
     The CORRECT filing sequence for the above names should be
     A. II, III, VI, V, IV, I   B. III, II, VI, V, IV, I
     C. VI, II, III, I, V, IV   D. III, II, VI, IV, V, I

Questions 35-40.

DIRECTIONS: Questions 35 through 40 are to be answered SOLELY on the basis of the following passage.

An aide assigned to the Complaint Room must be familiar with the various forms used by that office. Some of these forms and their uses are:

Complaint Report:	Used to record information on or information about crimes reported to the Police Department.
Complaint Report Follow-Up:	Used to record additional information after the initial complaint report has been filed
Aided Card:	Used to record information pertaining to sick and injured persons aided by the police.
Accident Report:	Used to record information on or information about injuries and/or property damage involving motorized vehicles.
Property Vouch:	Used to record information on or information about property which comes into possession of the Police Department. (Motorized vehicles are not included.)

Auto Voucher: Used to record information on or information about a motorized vehicle which comes into possession of the Police Department.

35. Mr. Brown walks into the police precinct and informs the Administrative Aide that, while he was at work, someone broke into his apartment and removed property belonging to him. He does not know everything that was taken, but he wants to make a report now and will make a list of what was taken and bring it in later.
According to the above passage, the CORRECT form to use in this situation should be the
   A. Property Voucher   B. Complaint Report
   C. Complaint Report Follow-Up   D. Aided Card

35.____

36. Mrs. Wilson telephones the precinct and informs the Administrative Aide she wishes to report additional property which was taken from her apartment. The Administrative Aide finds a Complaint Report had been previously filed for Mrs. Wilson.
According to the above passage, the CORRECT form to use in this situation should be the
   A. Property Voucher   B. Complaint Report
   C. Complaint Report Follow-Up   D. Aided Card

36.____

37. Police Officer Jones walks into the Complaint Room and informs the Administrative Aide that, while he was on patrol, he observed a woman fall to the sidewalk and remain there, apparently hurt. He comforted the injured woman and called for an ambulance, which came and brought the woman to the hospital.
According to the above passage, the CORRECT form on which to record this information should be the
   A. Accident Report   B. Complaint Report
   C. Complaint Report Follow-Up   D. Aided Card

37.____

38. Police Officer Smith informed the Administrative Aide assigned to the Complaint Room that Mr. Green, while crossing the street, was struck by a motorcycle and had to be taken to the hospital.
According to the above passage, the facts regarding this incident should be recorded on which one of the following forms?
   A. Accident Report   B. Complaint Report
   C. Complaint Report Follow-Up   D. Aided Card

38.____

39. Police Officer Williams reports to the Administrative Aide assigned to the Complaint Room that he and his partner, Police Officer Murphy, found an auto which was reported stolen and had the auto towed into the police garage.
Of the following forms listed in the above passage, which is the CORRECT one to use to record this information?
   A. Property Voucher   B. Auto Voucher
   C. Complaint Report Follow-Up   D. Complaint Report

39.____

40. Administrative Aide Lopez has been assigned to the Complaint Room. During her tour of duty, a person who does not identify herself hands Ms. Lopez a purse. The person states that she found the purse on the street. She then leaves the station house.
According to the information in the above passage, which is the CORRECT form to fill out to record the incident?
   A. Property Voucher
   B. Auto Voucher
   C. Complaint Report Follow-Up
   D. Complaint Report

KEY (CORRECT ANSWERS)

1.	B	11.	D	21.	A	31.	B
2.	D	12.	A	22.	C	32.	A
3.	B	13.	C	23.	A	33.	C
4.	C	14.	B	24.	C	34.	B
5.	A	15.	D	25.	A	35.	B
6.	D	16.	A	26.	A	36.	C
7.	C	17.	D	27.	D	37.	D
8.	A	18.	C	28.	C	38.	A
9.	C	19.	A	29.	D	39.	B
10.	B	20.	B	30.	B	40.	A

READING COMPREHENSION
UNDERSTANDING AND INTERPRETING WRITTEN MATERIAL
EXAMINATION SECTION
TEST 1

DIRECTIONS: The following questions are intended to test your ability to read with comprehension and to understand and interpret written materials, particularly legal passages. It will be necessary for you to read each paragraph carefully because the questions are based only on the material contained therein.
Each question has several suggested answers. *PRINT THE LETTER OF THE CORRECT ANSWER IN THE SPACE AT THE RIGHT.*

Questions 1-3.

DIRECTIONS: Answer Questions 1 to 3 SOLELY on the basis of the following statement:
   Foot patrol has some advantages over all other methods of patrol. Maximum opportunity is provided for observation within range of the senses and for close contact with people and things that enable the patrolman to provide a maximum service as an information source and counselor to the public and as the eyes and ears of the police department. A foot patrolman loses no time in alighting from a vehicle, and the performance of police tasks is not hampered by responsibility for his vehicle while afoot. Foot patrol, however, does not have many of the advantages of a patrol car. Lack of both mobility and immediate communication with headquarters lessens the officer's value in an emergency. The area that he can cover effectively is limited and, therefore, this method of patrol is costly.

1. According to this paragraph, the foot patrolman is the eyes and ears of the police department because he is

   A. in direct contact with the station house
   B. not responsible for a patrol vehicle
   C. able to observe closely conditions on his patrol post
   D. a readily available information source to the public

2. The MOST accurate of the following statements concerning the various methods of patrol, according to this paragraph, is that

   A. foot patrol should sometimes be combined with motor patrol
   B. foot patrol is better than motor patrol
   C. helicopter patrol has the same advantages as motor patrol
   D. motor patrol is more readily able to communicate with superior officers in an emergency

3. According to this paragraph, it is CORRECT to state that foot patrol is

   A. *economical* since increased mobility makes more rapid action possible
   B. *expensive* since the area that can be patrolled is relatively small
   C. *economical* since vehicle costs need not be considered
   D. *expensive* since giving information to the public is time-consuming

Questions 4-6.

DIRECTIONS: Answer Questions 4 to 6 SOLELY on the basis of the following statement:
All applicants for an original license to operate a catering establishment shall be fingerprinted. This shall include the officers, employees, and stockholders of the company and the members of a partnership. In case of a change, by addition or substitution, occurring during the existence of a license, the person added or substituted shall be fingerprinted. However, in the case of a hotel containing more than 200 rooms, only the officer or manager filing the application is required to be fingerprinted. The police commissioner may also at his discretion exempt the employees and stockholders of any company. The fingerprints shall be taken on one copy of form C.E. 20 and on two copies of C.E. 21. One copy of form C.E. 21 shall accompany the application. Fingerprints are not required with a renewal application.

4. According to this paragraph, an employee added to the payroll of a licensed catering establishment which is not in a hotel, must

   A. always be fingerprinted
   B. be fingerprinted unless he has been previously fingerprinted for another license
   C. be fingerprinted unless exempted by the police commissioner
   D. be fingerprinted only if he is the manager or an officer of the company

5. According to this paragraph, it would be MOST accurate to state that

   A. form C.E. 20 must accompany a renewal application
   B. form C.E. 21 must accompany all applications
   C. form C.E. 21 must accompany an original application
   D. both forms C.E. 20 and C.E. 21 must accompany all applications

6. A hotel of 270 rooms has applied for a license to operate a catering establishment on the premises. According to the instructions for fingerprinting given in this paragraph, the

   A. officers, employees, and stockholders shall be fingerprinted
   B. officers and manager shall be fingerprinted
   C. employees shall be fingerprinted
   D. officer filing the application shall be fingerprinted

Questions 7-9.

DIRECTIONS: Answer Questions 7 to 9 SOLELY on the basis of the following statement:
It is difficult to instill in young people inner controls on aggressive behavior in a world marked by aggression. The slum child's environment, full of hostility, stimulates him to delinquency; he does that which he sees about him. The time to act against delinquency is before it is committed. It is clear that juvenile delinquency, especially when it is committed in groups or gangs, leads almost inevitably to an adult criminal life unless it is checked at once. The first signs of vandalism and disregard for the comfort, health, and property of the community should be considered as storm warnings which cannot be ignored. The delinquent's first crime has the underlying element of testing the law and its ability to hit back.

7. A *suitable* title for this entire paragraph based on the material it contains is: 7.____

    A. The Need for Early Prevention of Juvenile Delinquency
    B. Juvenile Delinquency as a Cause of Slums
    C. How Aggressive Behavior Prevents Juvenile Delinquency
    D. The Role of Gangs in Crime

8. According to this paragraph, an *INITIAL* act of juvenile crime *usually* involves a(n) 8.____

    A. group or gang activity
    B. theft of valuable property
    C. test of the strength of legal authority
    D. act of physical violence

9. According to this paragraph, acts of juvenile delinquency are *most likely* to lead to a criminal career when they are 9.____

    A. acts of vandalism
    B. carried out by groups or gangs
    C. committed in a slum environment
    D. such as to impair the health of the neighborhood

Questions 10-12.

DIRECTIONS: Answer Questions 10 to 12 *SOLELY* on the basis of the following statement:
The police laboratory performs a valuable service in crime investigation by assisting in the reconstruction of criminal action and by aiding in the identification of persons and things. When studied by a technician, physical things found at crime scenes often reveal facts useful in identifying the criminal and in determining what has occurred. The nature of substances to be examined and the character of the examinations to be made vary so widely that the services of a large variety of skilled scientific persons are needed in crime investigations. To employ such a complete staff and to provide them with equipment and standards needed for all possible analyses and comparisons is beyond the means and the needs of any but the largest police departments. The search of crime scenes for physical evidence also calls for the services of specialists supplied with essential equipment and assigned to each tour of duty so as to provide service at any hour.

10. If a police department employs a large staff of technicians of various types in its laboratory, it will affect crime investigation to the extent that 10.____

    A. most crimes will be speedily solved
    B. identification of criminals will be aided
    C. search of crime scenes for physical evidence will become of less importance
    D. investigation by police officers will not usually be required

11. According to this paragraph, the *MOST* complete study of objects found at the scenes of crimes is 11.____

    A. always done in all large police departments
    B. based on assigning one technician to each tour of duty
    C. probably done only in large police departments
    D. probably done in police departments of communities with low crime rates

12. According to this paragraph, a large variety of skilled technicians is useful in criminal investigations because   12.___

    A. crimes cannot be solved without their assistance as a part of the police team
    B. large police departments need large staffs
    C. many different kinds of tests on various substances can be made
    D. the police cannot predict what methods may be tried by wily criminals

Questions 13-14.

DIRECTIONS: Answer Questions 13 and 14 SOLELY on the basis of the following statement:
The emotionally unstable person is always potentially a dangerous criminal, who causes untold misery to other persons and is a source of considerable trouble and annoyance to law enforcement officials. Like his fellow criminals he will be a menace to society as long as he is permitted to be at large. Police activities against him serve to sharpen his wits, and imprisonment gives him the opportunity to learn from others how to commit more serious crimes when he is released. This criminal's mental structure makes it impossible for him to profit by his experience with the police officials, by punishment of any kind or by sympathetic understanding and treatment by well-intentioned persons, professional and otherwise.

13. According to the above paragraph, the MOST accurate of the following statements concerning the relationship between emotional instability and crime is that   13.___

    A. emotional instability is proof of criminal activities
    B. the emotionally unstable person can become a criminal
    C. all dangerous criminals are emotionally unstable
    D. sympathetic understanding will prevent the emotionally unstable person from becoming a criminal

14. According to the above paragraph, the effect of police activities on the emotionally unstable criminal is that   14.___

    A. police activities aid this type of criminal to reform
    B. imprisonment tends to deter this type of criminal from committing future crimes
    C. contact with the police serves to assist sympathetic understanding and medical treatment
    D. police methods against this type of criminal develop him for further unlawful acts

Questions 15-17.

DIRECTIONS: Answer Questions 15 to 17 SOLELY on the basis of the following statement:
Proposals to license gambling operations are based on the belief that the human desire to gamble cannot be suppressed and, therefore, it should be licensed and legalized with the people sharing in the profits, instead of allowing the underworld to benefit. If these proposals are sincere, then it is clear that only one is worthwhile at all. Legalized gambling should be completely controlled and operated by the state with all the profits used for its citizens. A state agency should be set up to operate and control the gambling business. It should be as completely removed from politics as possible. In view of the inherent nature of the gambling business, with its close relationship to lawlessness and crime, only a man of the highest integrity should be eligible to become head of this agency. However, state gambling would encourage mass gambling with its attending social and economic evils in the same manner as other forms of legal gambling; but there is no justification whatever for the business of gambling to be legalized and then permitted to operate for private profit or for the benefit of any political organization.

15. The CENTRAL thought of this paragraph may be *correctly* expressed as the   15.____

    A. need to legalize gambling in the state
    B. state operation of gambling for the benefit of the people
    C. need to license private gambling establishments
    D. evils of gambling

16. According to this paragraph, a problem of legalized gambling which will *still* occur if the state operates the gambling business is   16.____

    A. the diversion of profits from gambling to private use
    B. that the amount of gambling will tend to diminish
    C. the evil effects of any form of mass gambling
    D. the use of gambling revenues for illegal purposes

17. According to this paragraph, to legalize the business of gambling would be   17.____

    A. *justified* because gambling would be operated only by a man of the highest integrity
    B. *justified* because this would eliminate politics
    C. *unjustified* under any conditions because the human desire to gamble cannot be suppressed
    D. *unjustified* if operated for private or political profit

Questions 18-20.

DIRECTIONS: Answer Questions 18 to 20 *SOLELY* on the basis of the following statement:
Whenever, in the course of the performance of their duties in an emergency, members of the force operate the emergency power switch at any location on the transit system and thereby remove power from portions of the track, or they are on the scene where this has been done, they will bear in mind that, although power is removed, further dangers exist; namely, that a train may coast into the area even though the power is off, or that the rails may be energized by a train which may be in a position to transfer electricity from a live portion of the third rail through its shoe beams. Employees must look in each direction before stepping upon, crossing, or standing close to tracks, being particularly careful not to come into contact with the third rail.

18. According to this paragraph, whenever an emergency occurs which has resulted in operating the emergency power switch, it is *MOST* accurate to state that   18.____

    A. power is shut off and employees may perform their duties in complete safety
    B. there may still be power in a portion of the third rail
    C. the switch will not operate if a portion of the track has been broken
    D. trains are not permitted to stop in the area of the emergency

19. An *important* precaution which this paragraph urges employees to follow after operating the emergency power switch, is to   19.____

    A. look carefully in both directions before stepping near the rails
    B. inspect the nearest train which has stopped to see if the power is on
    C. examine the third rail to see if the power is on
    D. check the emergency power switch to make sure it has operated properly

20. A trackman reports to you, a patrolman, that a dead body is lying on the road bed. You operate the emergency power switch. A train which has been approaching comes to a stop near the scene.
In order to act in accordance with the instructions in the above paragraph, you *should*

    A. climb down to the road bed and remove the body
    B. direct the train motorman to back up to the point where his train will not be in position to transfer electricity through its shoe beams
    C. carefully cross over the road bed to the body, avoiding the third rail and watching for train movements
    D. have the train motorman check to see if power is on before crossing to the tracks

21. The treatment to be given the offender cannot alter the fact of his offense; but we can take measures to reduce the chances of similar acts in the future. We should banish the criminal, not in order to exact revenge nor directly to encourage reform, but to deter him and others from further illegal attacks on society.
According to this paragraph, the *PRINCIPAL* reason for punishing criminals is to

    A. prevent the commission of future crimes
    B. remove them from society
    C. avenge society
    D. teach them that crime does not pay

22. Even the most comprehensive and best substantiated summaries of the total volume of criminal acts would not contribute greatly to an understanding of the varied social and biological factors which are sometimes assumed to enter into crime causation, nor would they indicate with any degree of precision the needs of police forces in combating crime.
According to this statement,

    A. crime statistics alone do not determine the needs of police forces in combating crime
    B. crime statistics are essential to a proper understanding of the social factors of crime
    C. social and biological factors which enter into crime causation have little bearing on police needs
    D. a knowledge of the social and biological factors of crime is essential to a proper understanding of crime statistics

23. The policeman's art consists of applying and enforcing a multitude of laws and ordinances in such degree or proportion and in such manner that the greatest degree of social protection will be secured. The degree of enforcement and the method of application will vary with each neighborhood and community.
According to the foregoing paragraph,

    A. each neighborhood or community must judge for itself to what extent the law is to be enforced
    B. a policeman should only enforce those laws which are designed to give the greatest degree of social protection
    C. the manner and intensity of law enforcement is not necessarily the same in all communities
    D. all laws and ordinances must be enforced in a community with the same degree of intensity

24. Police control in the sense of regulating the details of police operations, involves such matters as the technical means for so organizing the available personnel that competent police leadership, when secured, can operate effectively. It is concerned not so much with the extent to which popular controls can be trusted to guide and direct the course of police protection as with the administrative relationships which should exist between the component parts of the polie organism. According to the foregoing statement, police control is

    A. solely a matter of proper personnel assignment
    B. the means employed to guide and direct the course of police protection
    C. principally concerned with the administrative relationships between units of a police organization
    D. the sum total of means employed in rendering police protection

25. Police Department Rule 5 states that a Deputy Commissioner acting as Police Commissioner shall carry out the orders of the Police Commissioner, previously given, and such orders shall not, except in cases of extreme emergency, be countermanded. This means, most nearly, that, except in cases of extreme emergency,

    A. the orders given by a Deputy Commissioner acting as Police Commissioner may not be revoked
    B. a Deputy Commissioner acting as Police Commissioner should not revoke orders previously given by the Police Commissioner
    C. a Deputy Commissioner acting as Police Commissioner is vested with the same authority to issue orders as the Police Commissioner himself
    D. only a Deputy Commissioner acting as Police Commissioner may issue orders in the absence of the Police Commissioner himself

KEY (CORRECT ANSWERS)

1.	C	11.	C
2.	D	12.	C
3.	B	13.	B
4.	C	14.	D
5.	C	15.	B
6.	D	16.	C
7.	A	17.	D
8.	C	18.	B
9.	B	19.	A
10.	B	20.	C

21. A
22. A
23. C
24. C
25. B

TEST 2

Questions 1-2.

DIRECTIONS: Answer Questions 1 and 2 SOLELY on the basis of the following statement:
The medical examiner may contribute valuable data to the investigator of fires which cause fatalities. By careful examination of the bodies of any victims, he not only establishes cause of death, but may also furnish, in many instances, answers to questions relating to the identity of the victim and the source and origin of the fire. The medical examiner is of greatest value to law enforcement agencies because he is able to determine the exact cause of death through an examination of tissue of apparent arson victims. Thorough study of a burned body or even of parts of a burned body will frequently yield information which illuminates the problems confronting the arson investigator and the police.

1. According to the above paragraph, the MOST important task of the medical examiner in the investigation of arson is to obtain information concerning the

    A. identity of arsonists
    B. cause of death
    C. identity of victims
    D. source and origin of fires

2. The CENTRAL thought of the above paragraph is that the medical examiner aids in the solution of crimes of arson when

    A. a person is burnt to death
    B. identity of the arsonist is unknown
    C. the cause of the fire is known
    D. trained investigators are not available

Questions 3-6.

DIRECTIONS: Answer Questions 3 to 6 SOLELY on the basis of the following statement:
A foundling is an abandoned child whose identity is unknown. Desk officers shall direct the delivery, by a policewoman, if available, of foundlings actually or apparently under two years of age, to the Foundling Hospital, or if actually or apparently two years of age or over, to the Children's Center. In all other cases of dependent or neglected children, other than foundlings, requiring shelter, desk officers shall provide for obtaining such shelter as follows: between 9 a.m. and 5 p.m., Monday through Friday, by telephone direct to the Bureau of Child Welfare, in order to ascertain the shelter to which the child shall be sent; at all other times, direct the delivery of a child actually or apparently under two years of age to the Foundling Hospital, or, if the child is actually or apparently two years of age or over, to the Children's Center.

3. According to this paragraph, it would be MOST correct to state that

    A. a foundling as well as a neglected child may be delivered to the Foundling Hospital
    B. a foundling but not a neglected child may be delivered to the Children's Center
    C. a neglected child requiring shelter, regardless of age, may be delivered to the Bureau of Child Welfare
    D. the Bureau of Child Welfare may determine the shelter to which a foundling may be delivered

4. According to this paragraph, the desk officer shall provide for obtaining shelter for a neglected child, apparently under two years of age, by

   A. directing its delivery to the Children's Center if occurrence is on a Monday between 9 a.m. and 5 p.m.
   B. telephoning the Bureau of Child Welfare if occurrence is on a Sunday
   C. directing its delivery to the Foundling Hospital if occurrence is on a Wednesday at 4 p.m.
   D. telephoning the Bureau of Child Welfare if occurrence is at 10 a.m. on a Friday

4.____

5. According to this paragraph, the desk officer should direct delivery to the Foundling Hospital of any child who is

   A. actually under 2 years of age and requires shelter
   B. apparently under two years of age and is neglected or dependent
   C. actually 2 years of age and is a foundling
   D. apparently under 2 years of age and has been abandoned

5.____

6. A 12-year-old neglected child requiring shelter is brought to a police station on Thursday at 2 p.m. Such a child should be sent to

   A. a shelter selected by the Bureau of Child Welfare
   B. a shelter selected by the desk officer
   C. the Children's Center
   D. the Foundling Hospital when a brother or sister, under 2 years of age, also requires shelter

6.____

Questions 7-9.

DIRECTIONS: Answer Questions 7 to 9 SOLELY on the basis of the following statement:
   In addition to making the preliminary investigation of crimes, patrolmen should serve as eyes, ears, and legs for the detective division. The patrol division may be used for surveillance, to serve warrants and bring in suspects and witnesses, and to perform a number of routine tasks for the detectives which will increase the time available for tasks that require their special skills and facilities. It is to the advantage of individual detectives, as well as of the detective division, to have patrolmen working in this manner; more cases are cleared by arrest and a greater proportion of stolen property is recovered when, in addition to the detective regularly assigned, a number of patrolmen also work on the case. Detectives may stimulate the interest and participation of patrolmen by keeping them currently informed of the presence, identity, or description, hangouts, associates, vehicles and method of operation of each criminal known to be in the community.

7. According to this paragraph, a patrolman should

   A. assist the detective in certain of his routine functions
   B. be considered for assignment as a detective on the basis of his patrol performance
   C. leave the scene once a detective arrives
   D. perform as much of the detective's duties as time permits

7.____

8. According to this paragraph, patrolmen should aid detectives by

   A. accepting assignments from detectives which give promise of recovering stolen property
   B. making arrests of witnesses for the detective's interrogation
   C. performing all special investigative work for detectives
   D. producing for questioning individuals who may aid the detective in his investigation

9. According to this paragraph, detectives can keep patrolmen interested by

   A. ascertaining that patrolmen are doing investigative work properly
   B. having patrolmen directly under his supervision during an investigation
   C. informing patrolmen of the value of their efforts in crime prevention
   D. supplying the patrolmen with information regarding known criminals in the community

Questions 10-11.

DIRECTIONS: Answer Questions 10 and 11 SOLELY on the basis of the following statement:
State motor vehicle registration departments should and do play a vital role in the prevention and detection of automobile thefts. The combatting of theft is, in fact, one of the primary purposes of the registration of motor vehicles. As of recent date, there were approximately 61,309,000 motor vehicles registered in the United States. That same year some 200,000 of them were stolen. All but 6 percent have been or will be recovered. This is a very high recovery ratio compared to the percentage of recovery of other stolen personal property. The reason for this is that automobiles are carefully identified by the manufacturers and carefully registered by many of the states.

10. The CENTRAL thought of this paragraph is that there is a close relationship between the

    A. number of automobiles registered in the United States and the number stolen
    B. prevention of automobile thefts and the effectiveness of police departments in the United States
    C. recovery of stolen automobiles and automobile registration
    D. recovery of stolen automobiles and of other stolen property

11. According to this paragraph, the high recovery ratio for stolen automobiles is due to

    A. state registration and manufacturer identification of motor vehicles
    B. successful prevention of automobile thefts by state motor vehicle departments
    C. the fact that only 6% of stolen vehicles are not properly registered
    D. the high number of motor vehicles registered in the United States

Questions 12-15.

DIRECTIONS: Answer Questions 12 to 15 SOLELY on the basis of the following statement:
It is not always understood that the term "physical evidence" embraces any and all objects, living or inanimate. A knife, gun, signature, or burglar tool is immediately recognized as physical evidence. Less often is it considered that dust, microscopic fragments of all types, even an odor, may equally be physical evidence and often the most important of all. It is well established that the most useful types of physical evidence are generally microscopic in dimensions, that is, not noticeable by the eye and, therefore, most likely to be overlooked by

the criminal and by the investigator. For this reason, microscopic evidence persists for months or years after all other evidence has been removed and found inconclusive. Naturally, there are limitations to the time of collecting microscopic evidence as it may be lost or decayed. The exercise of judgment as to the possibility or profit of delayed action in collecting the evidence is a field in which the expert investigator should judge.

12. The *one* of the following which the above paragraph does *NOT* consider to be physical evidence is a

   A. criminal thought
   B. minute speck of dust
   C. raw onion smell
   D. typewritten note

13. According to the above paragraph, the re-checking of the scene of a crime

   A. is *useless* when performed years after the occurrence of the crime
   B. is *advisable* chiefly in crimes involving physical violence
   C. *may turn up* microscopic evidence of value
   D. *should be delayed* if the microscopic evidence is not subject to decay or loss

14. According to the above paragraph, the criminal investigator *should*

   A. give most of his attention to weapons used in the commission of the crime
   B. ignore microscopic evidence until a request is received from the laboratory
   C. immediately search for microscopic evidence and ignore the more visible objects
   D. realize that microscopic evidence can be easily overlooked

15. According to the above paragraph,

   A. a delay in collecting evidence must definitely diminish its value to the investigator
   B. microscopic evidence exists for longer periods of time than other physical evidence
   C. microscopic evidence is generally the most useful type of physical evidence
   D. physical evidence is likely to be overlooked by the criminal and by the investigator

Questions 16-18.

DIRECTIONS: Answer Questions 16 to 18 *SOLELY* on the basis of the following statement:
Sometimes, but not always, firing a gun leaves a residue of nitrate particles on the hands. This fact is utilized in the paraffin test which consists of applying melted paraffin and gauze to the fingers, hands, and wrists of a suspect until a cast of approximately 1/8 of an inch is built up. The heat of the paraffin causes the pores of the skin to open and release any particles embedded in them. The paraffin cast is then removed and tested chemically for nitrate particles. In addition to gunpowder, fertilizers, tobacco ashes, matches, and soot are also common sources of nitrates on the hands.

16. Assume that the paraffin test has been given to a person suspected of firing a gun and that nitrate particles have been found. It would be *CORRECT* to conclude that the suspect

   A. is guilty
   B. is innocent
   C. may be guilty or innocent
   D. is probably guilty

17. In testing for the presence of gunpowder particles on human hands, the characteristic of paraffin which makes it MOST serviceable is that it

   A. causes the nitrate residue left by a fired gun to adhere to the gauze
   B. is waterproof
   C. melts at a low temperature
   D. helps to distinguish between gunpowder nitrates and other types

18. According to the above paragraph, in the paraffin test, the nitrate particles are removed from the pores because the paraffin

   A. enlarges the pores
   B. contracts the pores
   C. reacts chemically with nitrates
   D. dissolves the particles

Questions 19-21.

DIRECTIONS: Answer Questions 19 to 21 SOLELY on the basis of the following statement:
Pickpockets operate most effectively when there are prospective victims in either heavily congested areas or in lonely places. In heavily populated areas, the large number of people about them covers the activities of these thieves. In lonely spots, they have the advantage of working unobserved. The main factor in the pickpocket's success is the selection of the "right" victim, A pickpocket's victim must, at the time of the crime, be inattentive, distracted, or unconscious. If any of these conditions exist, and if the pickpocket is skilled in his operations, the stage is set for a successful larceny. With the coming of winter, the crowds move southward – and so do most of the pickpockets. However, some pickpockets will remain in certain areas all year around. They will concentrate on theater districts, bus and railroad terminals, hotels or large shopping centers. A complete knowledge of the methods of this type of criminal and the ability to recognize them come only from long years of experience in performing patient surveillance and trailing of them. This knowledge is essential for the effective control and apprehension of this type of thief.

19. According to this paragraph, the pickpocket is LEAST likely to operate in a

   A. baseball park with a full capacity attendance
   B. station in an outlying area late at night
   C. moderately crowded dance hall
   D. over-crowded department store

20. According to this paragraph, the one of the following factors which is NOT necessary for the successful operation of the pickpocket is that

   A. he be proficient in the operations required to pick pockets
   B. the "right" potential victims be those who have been the subject of such a theft previously
   C. his operations be hidden from the view of others
   D. the potential victim be unaware of the actions of the pickpocket

21. According to this paragraph, it would be MOST correct to conclude that police officers who are successful in apprehending pickpockets

   A. are generallly those who have had lengthy experience in recognizing all types of criminals
   B. must, by intuition, be able to recognize potential "right" victims

C. must follow the pickpockets in their southward movement
D. must have acquired specific knowledge and skills in this field

Questions 22-23.

DIRECTIONS: Answer Questions 22 and 23 SOLELY on the basis of the following statement:
For many years, slums had been recognized as breeding disease, juvenile delinquency, and crime which not only threatened the health and welfare of the people who lived there, but also weakened the structure of society as a whole. As far back as 1834, a sanitary inspection report in the city pointed out the connection between insanitary, overcrowded housing and the spread of epidemics. Down through the years, evidence of slum-produced evils accumulated as the slums themselves continued to spread. This spread of slums was nationwide. Its symptoms and its ill effects were peculiar to no locality, but were characteristic of the country as a whole and imperiled the national welfare.

22. According to this paragraph, people who live in slum dwellings   22._____

    A. cause slums to become worse
    B. are threatened by disease and crime
    C. create bad housing
    D. are the chief source of crime in the country

23. According to this paragraph, the effects of juvenile delinquency and crime in slum areas were   23._____

    A. to destroy the structure of society
    B. noticeable in all parts of the country
    C. a chief cause of the spread of slums
    D. to spread insanitary conditions in the city

Questions 24-25.

DIRECTIONS: Questions 24 and 25 pertain to the following section of the Penal Law:
Section 1942. A person who, after having been three times convicted within this state, of felonies or attempts to commit felonies, or under the law of any other state, government or country, of crimes which if committed within this state would be felonious, commits a felony, other than murder, first or second degree, or treason, within this state, shall be sentenced upon conviction of such fourth, or subsequent, offense to imprisonment in a state prison for an indeterminate term the minimum of which shall be not less than the maximum term provided for first offenders for the crime for which the individual has been convicted, but, in any event, the minimum term upon conviction for a felony as the fourth, or subsequent, offense, shall be not less than fifteen years, and the maximum thereof shall be his natural life.

24. Under the terms of the above stated portion of Section 1942 of the Penal Law, a person must receive the increased punishment therein provided *if*   24._____

    A. he is convicted of a felony and has been three times previously convicted of felonies
    B. he has been three times previously convicted of felonies, regardless of the nature of his present conviction

C. his fourth conviction is for murder, first or second degree, or treason
D. he has previously been convicted three times of murder, first or second degree, or treason

25. Under the terms of the above stated portion of Section 1942 of the Penal Law, a person convicted of a felony for which the penalty is imprisonment for a term not to exceed ten years, and who has been three times previously convicted of felonies in this state, shall be sentenced to a term the *minimum* of which shall be

    A. ten years
    B. fifteen years
    C. indeterminate
    D. his natural life

25.____

KEY (CORRECT ANSWERS)

1.	B	11.	A
2.	A	12.	A
3.	A	13.	C
4.	D	14.	D
5.	D	15.	C
6.	A	16.	C
7.	A	17.	A
8.	D	18.	A
9.	D	19.	C
10.	C	20.	B

21.	D
22.	B
23.	B
24.	A
25.	B

RECORD KEEPING
EXAMINATION SECTION
TEST 1

DIRECTIONS: Each question or incomplete statement is followed by several suggested answers or completions. Select the one that BEST answers the question or completes the statement. *PRINT THE LETTER OF THE CORRECT ANSWER IN THE SPACE AT THE RIGHT.*

Questions 1-7.

DIRECTIONS: In answering Questions 1 through 7, use the following master list. For each question, determine where the name would fit on the master list. Each answer choice indicates right before or after the name in the answer choice.

    Aaron, Jane
    Armstead, Brendan
    Bailey, Charles
    Dent, Ricardo
    Grant, Mark
    Mars, Justin
    Methieu, Justine
    Parker, Cathy
    Sampson, Suzy
    Thomas, Heather

1. Schmidt, William
   A. Right before Cathy Parker
   B. Right after Heather Thomas
   C. Right after Suzy Sampson
   D. Right before Ricardo Dent

2. Asanti, Kendall
   A. Right before Jane Aaron
   B. Right after Charles Bailey
   C. Right before Justine Methieu
   D. Right after Brendan Armstead

3. O'Brien, Daniel
   A. Right after Justine Methieu
   B. Right before Jane Aaron
   C. Right after Mark Grant
   D. Right before Suzy Sampson

4. Marrow, Alison
   A. Right before Cathy Parker
   B. Right before Justin Mars
   C. Right before Mark Grant
   D. Right after Heather Thomas

5. Grantt, Marissa
   A. Right before Mark Grant
   B. Right after Mark Grant
   C. Right after Justin Mars
   D. Right before Suzy Sampson

6. Thompson, Heath
   A. Right after Justin Mars
   B. Right before Suzy Sampson
   C. Right after Heather Thomas
   D. Right before Cathy Parker

6._____

DIRECTIONS: Before answering Question 7, add in all of the names from Questions 1 through 6. Then fit the name in alphabetical order based on the new list.

7. Francisco, Mildred
   A. Right before Mark Grant
   B. Right after Marissa Grantt
   C. Right before Alison Marrow
   D. Right after Kendall Asanti

7._____

Questions 8-10.

DIRECTIONS: In answering Questions 8 through 10, compare each pair of names and addresses. Indicate whether they are the same or different in any way.

8. William H. Pratt, J.D.   William H. Pratt, J.D.
   Attourney at Law   Attorney at Law
   A. No differences
   B. 1 difference
   C. 2 differences
   D. 3 differences

8._____

9. 1303 Theater Drive,; Apt. 3-B   1330 Theatre Drive,; Apt. 3-B
   A. No differences
   B. 1 difference
   C. 2 differences
   D. 3 differences

9._____

10. Petersdorff, Briana and Mary   Petersdorff, Briana and Mary
    A. No differences
    B. 1 difference
    C. 2 differences
    D. 3 differences

10._____

11. Which of the following words, if any, are misspelled?
    A. Affordable
    B. Circumstansial
    C. Legalese
    D. None of the above

11._____

Questions 12-13.

DIRECTIONS: Questions 12 and 13 are to be answered on the basis of the following table.

Standardized Test Results for High School Students in District #1230

	English	Math	Science	Reading
High School 1	21	22	15	18
High School 2	12	16	13	15
High School 3	16	18	21	17
High School 4	19	14	15	16

The scores for each high school in the district were averaged out and listed for each subject tested. Scores of 0-10 are significantly below College Readiness Standards. 11-15 are below College Readiness, 16-20 meet College Readiness, and 21-25 are above College Readiness.

12. If the high schools need to meet or exceed in at least half the categories in order to NOT be considered "at risk," which schools are considered "at risk"?
    A. High School 2
    B. High School 3
    C. High School 4
    D. Both A and C

13. What percentage of subjects did the district as a whole meet or exceed College Readiness standards?
    A. 25%   B. 50%   C. 75%   D. 100%

Questions 14-15.

DIRECTIONS: Questions 14 and 15 are to be answered on the basis of the following information.

You have seven employees working as a part of your team: Austin, Emily, Jeremy, Christina, Martin, Harriet, and Steve. You have just sent an e-mail informing them that there will be a mandatory training session next week. To ensure that work still gets done, you are offering the training twice during the week: once on Tuesday and also on Thursday. This way half the employees will still be working while the other half attend the training. The only other issue is that Jeremy doesn't work on Tuesdays and Harriet doesn't work on Thursdays due to compressed work schedules.

14. Which of the following is a possible attendance roster for the first training session?
    A. Emily, Jeremy, Steve
    B. Steve, Christina, Harriet
    C. Harriet, Jeremy, Austin
    D. Steve, Martin, Jeremy

15. If Harriet, Christina, and Steve attend the training session on Tuesday, which of the following is a possible roster for Thursday's training session?
    A. Jeremy, Emily, and Austin
    B. Emily, Martin, and Harriet
    C. Austin, Christina, and Emily
    D. Jeremy, Emily, and Steve

Questions 16-20.

DIRECTIONS: In answering Questions 16 through 20, you will be given a word and will need to choose the answer choice that is MOST similar or different to the word.

16. Which word means the SAME as *annual*?
    A. Monthly   B. Usually   C. Yearly   D. Constantly

17. Which word means the SAME as *effort*?
    A. Energy   B. Equate   C. Cherish   D. Commence

18. Which word means the OPPOSITE of *forlorn*?
    A. Neglected   B. Lethargy   C. Optimistic   D. Astonished

19. Which word means the SAME as *risk*?
    A. Admire   B. Hazard   C. Limit   D. Hesitant

20. Which word means the OPPOSITE of *translucent*?
    A. Opaque   B. Transparent   C. Luminous   D. Introverted

21. Last year, Jamie's annual salary was $50,000. Her boss called her today to inform her that she would receive a 20% raise for the upcoming year. How much more money will Jamie receive next year?
    A. $60,000   B. $10,000   C. $1,000   D. $51,000

22. You and a co-worker work for a temp hiring agency as part of their office staff. You both are given 6 days off per month. How many days off are you and your co-worker given in a year?
    A. 24   B. 72   C. 144   D. 48

23. If Margot makes $34,000 per year and she works 40 hours per week for all 52 weeks, what is her hourly rate?
    A. $16.34/hour   B. $17.00/hour   C. $15.54/hour   D. $13.23/hour

24. How many dimes are there in $175.00?
    A. 175   B. 1,750   C. 3,500   D. 17,500

25. If Janey is three times as old as Emily, and Emily is 3, how old is Janey?
    A. 6   B. 9   C. 12   D. 15

KEY (CORRECT ANSWERS)

1.	C		11.	B
2.	D		12.	A
3.	A		13.	D
4.	B		14.	B
5.	B		15.	A
6.	C		16.	C
7.	A		17.	A
8.	B		18.	C
9.	C		19.	B
10.	A		20.	A

21. B
22. C
23. A
24. B
25. B

TEST 2

DIRECTIONS: Each question or incomplete statement is followed by several suggested answers or completions. Select the one that BEST answers the question or completes the statement. *PRINT THE LETTER OF THE CORRECT ANSWER IN THE SPACE AT THE RIGHT.*

Questions 1-6.

DIRECTIONS: Questions 1 through 6 are to be answered on the basis of the following information.

item	name of item to be ordered
quantity	minimum number that can be ordered
beginning amount	amount in stock at start of month
amount received	amount receiving during month
ending amount	amount in stock at end of month
amount used	amount used during month
amount to order	will need at least as much of each item as used in the previous month
unit price	cost of each unit of an item
total price	total price for the order

Item	Quantity	Beginning	Received	Ending	Amount Used	Amount to Order	Unit Price	Total Price
Pens	10	22	10	8	24	20	$0.11	$2.20
Spiral notebooks	8	30	13	12			$0.25	
Binder clips	2 boxes	3 boxes	1 box	1 box			$1.79	
Sticky notes	3 packs	12 packs	4 packs	2 packs			$1.29	
Dry erase markers	1 pack (dozen)	34 markers	8 markers	40 markers			$16.49	
Ink cartridges (printer)	1 cartridge	3 cartridges	1 cartridge	2 cartridges			$79.99	
Folders	10 folders	25 folders	15 folders	10 folders			$1.08	

1. How many packs of sticky notes were used during the month?   1.____
    A. 16   B. 10   C. 12   D. 14

2. How many folders need to be ordered for next month?   2.____
    A. 15   B. 20   C. 30   D. 40

3. What is the total price of notebooks that you will need to order?   3.____
    A. $6.00   B. $0.25   C. $4.50   D. $2.75

4. Which of the following will you spend the second most money on?   4.____
    A. Ink cartridges   B. Dry erase markers
    C. Sticky notes   D. Binder clips

5. How many packs of dry erase markers should you order?   5.____
    A. 1   B. 8   C. 12   D. 0

95

6. What will be the total price of the file folders you order? 6._____
   A. $20.16   B. $21.60   C. $10.80   D. $4.32

Questions 7-11.

DIRECTIONS: Questions 7 through 11 are to be answered on the basis of the following table.

Number of Car Accidents, By Location and Cause, for 2014						
	Location 1		Location 2		Location 3	
Cause	Number	Percent	Number	Percent	Number	Percent
Severe Weather	10		25		30	
Excessive Speeding	20	40	5		10	
Impaired Driving	15		15	25	8	
Miscellaneous	5		15		2	4
TOTALS	50	100	60	100	50	100

7. Which of the following is the third highest cause of accidents for all three locations? 7._____
   A. Severe Weather   B. Impaired Driving
   C. Miscellaneous   D. Excessive Speeding

8. The average number of Severe Weather accidents per week at Location 3 for the year (52 weeks) was MOST NEARLY 8._____
   A. 0.57   B. 30   C. 1   D. 1.25

9. Which location had the LARGEST percentage of accidents caused by Impaired Driving? 9._____
   A. 1   B. 2   C. 3   D. Both A and B

10. If one-third of the accidents at all three locations resulted in at least one fatality, what is the LEAST amount of deaths caused by accidents last year? 10._____
    A. 60   B. 106   C. 66   D. 53

11. What is the percentage of accidents caused by miscellaneous means from all three locations in 2014? 11._____
    A. 5%   B. 10%   C. 13%   D. 25%

12. How many pairs of the following groups of letters are exactly alike? 12._____
    ACDOBJ   ACDBOJ
    HEWBWR   HEWRWB
    DEERVS   DEERVS
    BRFQSX   BRFQSX
    WEYRVB   WEYRVB
    SPQRZA   SQRPZA

    A. 2   B. 3   C. 4   D. 5

Questions 13-19.

DIRECTIONS: Questions 13 through 19 are to be answered on the basis of the following information.

In 2012, the most current information on the American population was finished. The information was compiled by 200 volunteers in each of the 50 states. The territory of Puerto Rico, a sovereign of the United States, had 25 people assigned to compile data. In February of 2010, volunteers in each state and sovereign began collecting information. In Puerto Rico, data collection finished by January 31st, 2011, while work in the United States was completed on June 30, 2012. Each volunteer gathered data on the population of their state or sovereign. When the information was compiled, volunteers sent reports to the nation's capital, Washington, D.C. Each volunteer worked 20 hours per month and put together 10 reports per month. After the data was compiled in total, 50 people reviewed the data and worked from January 2012 to December 2012.

13. How many reports were generated from February 2010 to April 2010 in Illinois and Ohio?
    A. 3,000   B. 6,000   C. 12,000   D. 15,000

14. How many volunteers in total collected population data in January 2012?
    A. 10,000   B. 2,000   C. 225   D. 200

15. How many reports were put together in May 2012?
    A. 2,000   B. 50,000   C. 100,000   D. 100,250

16. How many hours did the Puerto Rican volunteers work in the fall (September-November)?
    A. 60   B. 500   C. 1,500   D. 0

17. How many workers were compiling or reviewing data in July 2012?
    A. 25   B. 50   C. 200   D. 250

18. What was the total amount of hours worked by Nevada volunteers in July 2010?
    A. 500   B. 4,000   C. 4,500   D. 5,000

19. How many reviewers worked in January 2013?
    A. 75   B. 50   C. 0   D. 25

20. John has to file 10 documents per shelf. How many documents would it take for John to fill 40 shelves?
    A. 40   B. 400   C. 4,500   D. 5,000

21. Jill wants to travel from New York City to Los Angeles by bike, which is approximately 2,772 miles. How many miles per day would Jill need to average if she wanted to complete the trip in 4 weeks?
    A. 100   B. 89   C. 99   D. 94

4 (#2)

22. If there are 24 CPU's and only 7 monitors, how many more monitors do you need to have the same amount of monitors as CPU's? 22.____
    A. Not enough information   B. 17
    C. 31   D. 0

23. If Gerry works 5 days a week and 8 hours each day, and John works 3 days a week and 10 hours each day, how many more hours per year will Gerry work than John? 23.____
    A. They work the same amount of hours.
    B. 450
    C. 520
    D. 832

24. Jimmy gets transferred to a new office. The new office has 25 employees, but only 16 are there due to a blizzard. How many coworkers was Jimmy able to meet on his first day? 24.____
    A. 16   B. 25   C. 9   D. 7

25. If you do a fundraiser for charities in your area and raise $500 total, how much would you give to each charity if you were donating equal amounts to 3 of them? 25.____
    A. $250.00   B. $167.77   C. $50.00   D. $111.11

KEY (CORRECT ANSWERS)

1. D   11. C
2. B   12. B
3. A   13. C
4. C   14. A
5. D   15. C

6. B   16. C
7. D   17. B
8. A   18. B
9. A   19. C
10. D   20. B

21. C
22. B
23. C
24. A
25. B

TEST 3

DIRECTIONS: Each question or incomplete statement is followed by several suggested answers or completions. Select the one that BEST answers the question or completes the statement. *PRINT THE LETTER OF THE CORRECT ANSWER IN THE SPACE AT THE RIGHT.*

Questions 1-3.

DIRECTIONS: In answering Questions 1 through 3, choose the correctly spelled word.

1. A. allusion   B. alusion   C. allusien   D. allution   1.____
2. A. altitude   B. alltitude   C. atlitude   D. altlitude   2.____
3. A. althogh   B. allthough   C. althrough   D. although   3.____

Questions 4-9.

DIRECTIONS: In answering Questions 4 through 9, choose the answer that BEST completes the analogy.

4. Odometer is to mileage as compass is to   4.____
   A. speed   B. needle   C. hiking   D. direction

5. Marathon is to race as hibernation is to   5.____
   A. winter   B. dream   C. sleep   D. bear

6. Cup is to coffee as bowl is to   6.____
   A. dish   B. spoon   C. food   D. soup

7. Flow is to river as stagnant is to   7.____
   A. pool   B. rain   C. stream   D. canal

8. Paw is to cat as hoof is to   8.____
   A. lamb   B. horse   C. lion   D. elephant

9. Architect is to building as sculptor is to   9.____
   A. museum   B. chisel   C. stone   D. statue

Questions 10-14.

DIRECTIONS: Questions 10 through 14 are to be answered on the basis of the following graph.

Population of Carroll City Broken Down by Age and Gender (in Thousands)			
Age	Female	Male	Total
Under 15	60	60	120
15-23		22	
24-33		20	44
34-43	13	18	31
44-53	20		67
64 and Over	65	65	130
TOTAL	230	232	462

10. How many people in the city are between the ages of 15-23?
    A. 70
    B. 46,000
    C. 70,000
    D. 225,000

11. Approximately what percentage of the total population of the city was female aged 24-33?
    A. 10%
    B. 5%
    C. 15%
    D. 25%

12. If 33% of the males have a job and 55% of females don't have a job, which of the following statements is TRUE?
    A. Males have approximately 2,600 more jobs than females.
    B. Females have approximately 49,000 more jobs than males.
    C. Females have approximately 26,000 more jobs than males.
    D. None of the above statements are true.

13. How many females between the ages of 15-23 live in Carroll City?
    A. 67,000
    B. 24,000
    C. 48,000
    D. 91,000

14. Assume all males 44-53 living in Carroll City are employed. If two-thirds of males age 44-53 work jobs outside of Carroll City, how many work within city limits?
    A. 31,333
    B. 15,667
    C. 47,000
    D. Cannot answer the question with the information provided

Questions 15-16.

DIRECTIONS: Questions 15 and 16 are labeled as shown. Alphabetize them for filing. Choose the answer that correctly shows the order.

15. (1) AED
    (2) OOS
    (3) FOA
    (4) DOM
    (5) COB

    A. 2-5-4-3-2 B. 1-4-5-2-3 C. 1-5-4-2-3 D. 1-5-4-3-2

16. Alphabetize the names of the people. Last names are given last.
    (1) Lindsey Jamestown
    (2) Jane Alberta
    (3) Ally Jamestown
    (4) Allison Johnston
    (5) Lyle Moreno

    A. 2-1-3-4-5 B. 3-4-2-1-5 C. 2-3-1-4-5 D. 4-3-2-1-5

17. Which of the following words is misspelled?
    A. disgust
    B. whisper
    C. locale
    D. none of the above

Questions 18-21.

DIRECTIONS: Questions 18 through 21 are to be answered on the basis of the following list of employees.

    Robertson, Aaron
    Bacon, Gina
    Jerimiah, Trace
    Gillette, Stanley
    Jacks, Sharon

18. Which employee name would come in third in alphabetized list?
    A. Robertson, Aaron
    B. Jerimiah, Trace
    C. Gillette, Stanley
    D. Jacks, Sharon

19. Which employee's first name starts with the letter in the alphabet that is five letters after the first letter of their last name?
    A. Jerimiah, Trace
    B. Bacon, Gina
    C. Jacks, Sharon
    D. Gillette, Stanley

20. How many employees have last names that are exactly five letters long?
    A. 1 B. 2 C. 3 D. 4

21. How many of the employees have either a first or last name that starts with the letter "G"?
    A. 1   B. 2   C. 4   D. 5

Questions 22-25.

DIRECTIONS: Questions 22 through 25 are to be answered on the basis of the following chart.

Bicycle Sales (Model #34JA32)							
Country	May	June	July	August	September	October	Total
Germany	34	47	45	54	56	60	296
Britain	40	44	36	47	47	46	260
Ireland	37	32	32	32	34	33	200
Portugal	14	14	14	16	17	14	89
Italy	29	29	28	31	29	31	177
Belgium	22	24	24	26	25	23	144
Total	176	198	179	206	208	207	1166

22. What percentage of the overall total was sold to the German importer?
    A. 25.3%   B. 22%   C. 24.1%   D. 23%

23. What percentage of the overall total was sold in September?
    A. 24.1%   B. 25.6%   C. 17.9%   D. 24.6%

24. What is the average number of units per month imported into Belgium over the first four months shown?
    A. 26   B. 20   C. 24   D. 31

25. If you look at the three smallest importers, what is their total import percentage?
    A. 35.1%   B. 37.1%   C. 40%   D. 28%

KEY (CORRECT ANSWERS)

1. A
2. A
3. D
4. D
5. C

6. D
7. A
8. B
9. D
10. C

11. B
12. C
13. C
14. B
15. D

16. C
17. D
18. D
19. B
20. B

21. B
22. A
23. C
24. C
25. A

TEST 4

DIRECTIONS: Each question or incomplete statement is followed by several suggested answers or completions. Select the one that BEST answers the question or completes the statement. *PRINT THE LETTER OF THE CORRECT ANSWER IN THE SPACE AT THE RIGHT.*

Questions 1-6.

DIRECTIONS: In answering Questions 1 through 6, choose the sentence that represents the BEST example of English grammar.

1. A. Joey and me want to go on a vacation next week.
    B. Gary told Jim he would need to take some time off.
    C. If turning six years old, Jim's uncle would teach Spanish to him.
    D. Fax a copy of your resume to Ms. Perez and me.

2. A. Jerry stood in line for almost two hours.
    B. The reaction to my engagement was less exciting than I thought it would be.
    C. Carlos and me have done great work on this project.
    D. Two parts of the speech needs to be revised before tomorrow.

3. A. Arriving home, the alarm was tripped.
    B. Jonny is regarded as a stand up guy, a responsible parent, and he doesn't give up until a task is finished.
    C. Each employee must submit a drug test each month.
    D. One of the documents was incinerated in the explosion.

4. A. As soon as my parents get home, I told them I finished all of my chores.
    B. I asked my teacher to send me my missing work, check my absences, and how did I do on my test.
    C. Matt attempted to keep it concealed from Jenny and me.
    D. If Mary or him cannot get work done on time, I will have to split them up.

5. A. Driving to work, the traffic report warned him of an accident on Highway 47.
    B. Jimmy has performed well this season.
    C. Since finishing her degree, several job offers have been given to Cam.
    D. Our boss is creating unstable conditions for we employees.

6. A. The thief was described as a tall man with a wiry mustache weighing approximately 150 pounds.
    B. She gave Patrick and I some more time to finish our work.
    C. One of the books that he ordered was damaged in shipping.
    D. While talking on the rotary phone, the car Jim was driving skidded off the road.

Questions 7-9.

DIRECTIONS: Questions 7 through 9 are to be answered on the basis of the following graph.

Ice Lake Frozen Flight (2002-2013)		
Year	Number of Participants	Temperature (Fahrenheit)
2002	22	4°
2003	50	33°
2004	69	18°
2005	104	22°
2006	108	24°
2007	288	33°
2008	173	9°
2009	598	39°
2010	698	26°
2011	696	30°
2012	777	28°
2013	578	32°

7. Which two year span had the LARGEST difference between temperatures?
    A. 2002 and 2003
    B. 2011 and 2012
    C. 2008 and 2009
    D. 2003 and 2004

8. How many total people participated in the years after the temperature reached at least 29°?
    A. 2,295   B. 1,717   C. 2,210   D. 4,543

9. In 2007, the event saw 288 participants, while in 2008 that number dropped to 173. Which of the following reasons BEST explains the drop in participants?
    A. The event had not been going on that long and people didn't know about it.
    B. The lake water wasn't cold enough to have people jump in.
    C. The temperature was too cold for many people who would have normally participated.
    D. None of the above reasons explain the drop in participants.

10. In the following list of numbers, how many times does 4 come just after 2 when 2 comes just after an odd number?
    2365247653898632488572486392424
    A. 2   B. 3   C. 4   D. 5

11. Which choice below lists the letter that is as far after B as S is after N in the alphabet?
    A. G   B. H   C. I   D. J

Questions 12-15.

DIRECTIONS: Questions 12 through 15 are to be answered on the basis of the following directory and list of changes.

Directory		
Name	Emp. Type	Position
Julie Taylor	Warehouse	Packer
James King	Office	Administrative Assistant
John Williams	Office	Salesperson
Ray Moore	Warehouse	Maintenance
Kathleen Byrne	Warehouse	Supervisor
Amy Jones	Office	Salesperson
Paul Jonas	Office	Salesperson
Lisa Wong	Warehouse	Loader
Eugene Lee	Office	Accountant
Bruce Lavine	Office	Manager
Adam Gates	Warehouse	Packer
Will Suter	Warehouse	Packer
Gary Lorper	Office	Accountant
Jon Adams	Office	Salesperson
Susannah Harper	Office	Salesperson

Directory Updates:
- Employee e-mail addresses will adhere to the following guidelines: lastnamefirstname@apexindustries.com (ex. Susannah Harper is harpersusannah@apexindustries.com). Currently, employees in the warehouse share one e-mail, distribution@apexindustries.com.
- The "Loader" position will now be referred to as "Specialist I"
- Adam Gates has accepted a Supervisor position within the Warehouse and is no longer a Packer. All warehouse employees report to the two Supervisors and all office employees report to the Manager.

12. Amy Jones tried to send an e-mail to Adam Gates, but it wouldn't send. Which of the following offers the BEST explanation?
    A. Amy put Adam's first name first and then his last name.
    B. Adam doesn't check his e-mail, so he wouldn't know if he received the e-mail or not.
    C. Adam does not have his own e-mail.
    D. Office employees are not allowed to send e-mails to each other.

13. How many Packers currently work for Apex Industries?
    A. 2   B. 3   C. 4   D. 5

14. What position does Lisa Wong currently hold?
    A. Specialist I   B. Secretary
    C. Administrative Assistant   D. Loader

15. If an employee wanted to contact the office manager, which of the following e-mails should the e-mail be sent to?   15.____
    A. officemanager@apexindustries.com
    B. brucelavine@apexindustries.com
    C. lavinebruce@apexindustries.com
    D. distribution@apexindustries.com

Questions 16-19.

DIRECTIONS: In answering Questions 16 through 19, compare the three names, numbers or addresses.

16. Smiley Yarnell   Smiley Yarnel   Smily Yarnell   16.____
    A. All three are exactly alike.
    B. The first and second are exactly alike.
    C. The second and third are exactly alike.
    D. All three are different.

17. 1583 Theater Drive   1583 Theater Drive   1583 Theatre Drive   17.____
    A. All three are exactly alike.
    B. The first and second are exactly alike.
    C. The second and third are exactly alike.
    D. All three are different.

18. 3341893212   3341893212   3341893212   18.____
    A. All three are exactly alike.
    B. The first and second are exactly alike.
    C. The second and third are exactly alike.
    D. All three are different.

19. Douglass Watkins   Douglas Watkins   Douglass Watkins   19.____
    A. All three are exactly alike.
    B. The first and third are exactly alike.
    C. The second and third are exactly alike.
    D. All three are different.

Questions 20-24.

DIRECTIONS: In answering Questions 20 through 24, you will be presented with a word. Choose the synonym that BEST represents the word in question.

20. Flexible   20.____
    A. delicate   B. inflammable   C. strong   D. pliable

21. Alternative   21.____
    A. choice   B. moderate   C. lazy   D. value

22. Corroborate
    A. examine   B. explain   C. verify   D. explain   22._____

23. Respiration
    A. recovery   B. breathing   C. sweating   D. selfish   23._____

24. Negligent
    A. lazy   B. moderate   C. hopeless   D. lax   24._____

25. Plumber is to Wrench as Painter is to
    A. pipe   B. shop   C. hammer   D. brush   25._____

KEY (CORRECT ANSWERS)

1. D
2. A
3. D
4. C
5. B

6. C
7. C
8. B
9. C
10. C

11. A
12. C
13. A
14. A
15. C

16. D
17. B
18. A
19. B
20. D

21. A
22. C
23. B
24. D
25. D

CLERICAL ABILITIES TEST
EXAMINATION SECTION
TEST 1

DIRECTIONS: Each question or incomplete statement is followed by several suggested answers or completions. Select the one that BEST answers the question or completes the statement. *PRINT THE LETTER OF THE CORRECT ANSWER IN THE SPACE AT THE RIGHT.*

Questions 1-10.

DIRECTIONS: Questions 1 through 10 consist of lines of names, dates, and numbers. For each question, you are to choose the option (A, B, C, or D) in Column II which EXACTLY matches the information in Column I. *PRINT THE LETTER OF THE CORRECT ANSWER IN THE SPACE AT THE RIGHT.*

SAMPLE QUESTION

Column I
Schneider 11/16/75 581932

Column II
A. Schneider 11/16/75 518932
B. Schneider 11/16/75 581932
C. Schnieder 11/16/75 581932
D. Shnieder 11/16/75 518932

The correct answer is B. Only Option B shows the name, date, and number exactly as they are in Column I. Option A has a mistake in the number. Option C has a mistake in the name. Option D has a mistake in the name and in the number. Now answer Questions 1 through 10 in the same manner.

Column I
1. Johnston 12/26/74 659251

Column II
A. Johnson 12/23/74 659251
B. Johston 12/26/74 659251
C. Johnston 12/26/74 695251
D. Johnston 12/26/74 659251

1._____

2. Allison 1/26/75 9939256

A. Allison 1/26/75 9939256
B. Alisson 1/26/75 9939256
C. Allison 1/26/76 9399256
D. Allison 1/26/75 9993356

2._____

3. Farrell 2/12/75 361251

A. Farell 2/21/75 361251
B. Farrell 2/12/75 361251
C. Farrell 2/21/75 361251
D. Farrell 2/12/75 361151

3._____

4. Guerrero 4/28/72 105689
    A. Guererro 4/28/72 105689
    B. Guererro 4/28/72 105986
    C. Guererro 4/28/72 105869
    D. Guerrero 4/28/72 105689

    4.____

5. McDonnell 6/05/73 478215
    A. McDonnell 6/15/73 478215
    B. McDonnell 6/05/73 478215
    C. McDonnell 6/05/73 472815
    D. MacDonell 6/05/73 478215

    5.____

6. Shepard 3/31/71 075421
    A. Sheperd 3/31/71 075421
    B. Shepard 3/13/71 075421
    C. Shepard 3/31/71 075421
    D. Shepard 3/13/71 075241

    6.____

7. Russell 4/01/69 031429
    A. Russell 4/01/69 031429
    B. Russell 4/10/69 034129
    C. Russell 4/10/69 031429
    D. Russell 4/01/69 034129

    7.____

8. Phillips 10/16/68 961042
    A. Philipps 10/16/68 961042
    B. Phillips 10/16/68 960142
    C. Phillips 10/16/68 961042
    D. Philipps 10/16/68 916042

    8.____

9. Campbell 11/21/72 624856
    A. Campbell 11/21/72 624856
    B. Campbell 11/21/72 624586
    C. Campbell 11/21/72 624686
    D. Campbel 11/21/72 624856

    9.____

10. Patterson 9/18/71 76199176
    A. Patterson 9/18/72 76191976
    B. Patterson 9/18/71 76199176
    C. Patterson 9/18/72 76199176
    D. Patterson 9/18/71 76919176

    10.____

Questions 11-15.

DIRECTIONS: Questions 11 through 15 consist of groups of numbers and letters which you are to compare. For each question, you are to choose the option (A, B, C, or D) in Column I which EXACTLY matches the group of numbers and letters given in Column I.

SAMPLE QUESTION

Column I
B92466

Column II
A. B92644
B. B94266
C. A92466
D. B92466

The correct answer is D. Only Option D in Column II shows the group of numbers and letters EXACTLY as it appears in Column I. Now answer Questions 11 through 15 in the same manner.

Column I
11. 925AC5

Column II
A. 952CA5
B. 925AC5
C. 952AC5
D. 925CA6

11.____

12. Y006925

A. Y060925
B. Y006295
C. Y006529
D. Y006925

12.____

13. J236956

A. J236956
B. J326965
C. J239656
D. J932656

13.____

14. AB6952

A. AB6952
B. AB9625
C. AB9652
D. AB6925

14.____

15. X259361

A. X529361
B. X259631
C. X523961
D. X259361

15.____

Questions 16-25.

DIRECTIONS: Each of questions 16 through 25 consists of three lines of code letters and three lines of numbers. The numbers on each line should correspond with the code letters on the same line in accordance with the table below.

Code Letter	S	V	W	A	Q	M	X	E	G	K
Corresponding Number	0	1	2	3	4	5	5	7	8	9

On some of the lines, an error exists in the coding. Compare the letters and numbers in each question carefully. If you find an error or errors on:
    only one of the lines in the question, mark your answer A;
    any two lines in the question, mark your answer B;
    all three lines in the question, mark your answer C;
    none of the lines in the question, mark your answer D.

4 (#1)

SAMPLE QUESTION

WQGKSXG   2489068
XEKVQMA   6591453
KMAESXV   9527061

In the above sample, the first line is correct since each code letter listed has the correct corresponding number. On the second line, an error exists because code letter E should have the number 7 instead of the number 5. On the third line, an error exists because the code letter A should have the number 3 instead of the number 2. Since there are errors in two of the three lines, the correct answer is B. Now answer Questions 16 through 25 in the same manner.

16. SWQEKGA   0247983   16._____
    KEAVSXM   9731065
    SSAXGKQ   0036894

17. QAMKMVS   4259510   17._____
    MGGEASX   5897306
    KSWMKWS   9125920

18. WKXQWVE   2964217   18._____
    QKXXQVA   4966413
    AWMXGVS   3253810

19. GMMKASE   8559307   19._____
    AWVSKSW   3210902
    QAVSVGK   4310189

20. XGKQSMK   6894049   20._____
    QSVKEAS   4019730
    GSMXKMV   8057951

21. AEKMWSG   3195208   21._____
    MKQSVQK   5940149
    XGQAEVW   6843712

22. XGMKAVS   6858310   22._____
    SKMAWEQ   0953174
    GVMEQSA   8167403

23. VQSKAVE   1489317   23._____
    WQGKAEM   2489375
    MEGKAWQ   5689324

24. XMQVSKG   6541098   24._____
    QMEKEWS   4579720
    KMEVGKG   9571983

25. GKVAMEW   88912572   25.____
    AXMVKAE   3651937
    KWAGMAV   9238531

Questions 26-35.

DIRECTIONS: Each of Questions 26 through 35 consists of a column of figures. For each question, add the column of figures and choose the correct answer from the four choices given.

26. 5,665.43   26.____
    2,356.69
    6,447.24
    7,239.65

    A. 20,698.01   B. 21,709.01
    C. 21,718.01   D. 22,609.01

27. 817,209.55   27.____
    264,354.29
     82,368.76
    849,964.89

    A. 1,893.977.49   B. 1,989,988.39
    C. 2,009,077.39   D. 2,013,897.49

28. 156,366.89   28.____
    249,973.23
    823,229.49
     56,869.45

    A. 1,286,439.06   B. 1,287,521.06
    C. 1,297,539.06   D. 1,296,421.06

29. 23,422.15   29.____
    149,696.24
    238,377.53
     86,289.79
    505,533.63

    A. 989,229.34   B. 999,879.34
    C. 1,003,330.34   D. 1,023,329.34

6 (#1)

30.   2,468,926.70
       656,842.28
        49,723.15
       832,369.59

    A. 3,218,062.72   B. 3,808,092.72
    C. 4,007,861.72   D. 4,818,192.72

30.____

31.   524,201.52
    7,775,678.51
    8,345,299.63
  40,628,898.08
  31,374,670.07

    A. 88,646,647.81   B. 88,646,747.91
    C. 88,648,647.91   D. 88,648,747.81

31.____

32.   6,824,829.40
     682,482.94
  5,542,015.27
     775,678.51
  7,732,507.25

    A. 21,557,513.37   B. 21,567,513.37
    C. 22,567,503.37   D. 22,567,513.37

32.____

33.   22,109,405.58
    6,097,093.43
    5,050,073.99
    8,118,050.05
    4,313,980.82

    A. 45,688,593.87   B. 45,688,603.87
    C. 45,689,593.87   D. 45,689,603.87

33.____

34.   79,324,114.19
    99,848,129.74
    43,331,653.31
    41,610,207.14

    A. 264,114,104.38   B. 264,114,114.38
    C. 265,114,114.38   D. 265,214,104.38

34.____

35. 33,729,653.94
    5,959,342.58
   26,052,715.47
    4,452,669.52
    7,079,953.59

   A. 76,374,334.10
   C. 77,274,335.10
   B. 76,375,334.10
   D. 77,275,335.10

35.____

Questions 36-40.

DIRECTIONS: Each of Questions 36 through 40 consists of a single number in Column I and four options in Column II. For each question, you are to choose the option (A, B, C, or D) in Column II which EXACTLY matches the number in Column I.

SAMPLE QUESTION

Column I
5965121

Column II
A. 5956121
B. 5965121
C. 5966121
D. 5965211

The correct answer is B. Only Option B shows the number EXACTLY as it appears in Column I. Now answer Questions 36 through 40 in the same manner.

Column I
36. 9643242

Column II
A. 9643242
B. 9462342
C. 9642442
D. 9463242

36.____

37. 3572477

A. 3752477
B. 3725477
C. 3572477
D. 3574277

37.____

38. 5276101

A. 5267101
B. 5726011
C. 5271601
D. 5276101

38.____

39. 4469329

A. 4496329
B. 4469329
C. 4496239
D. 4469239

39.____

40. 2326308

A. 2236308
B. 2233608
C. 2326308
D. 2323608

40. ____

KEY (CORRECT ANSWERS)

1.	D	11.	B	21.	A	31.	D
2.	A	12.	D	22.	C	32.	A
3.	B	13.	A	23.	B	33.	B
4.	D	14.	A	24.	D	34.	A
5.	B	15.	D	25.	A	35.	C
6.	C	16.	D	26.	B	36.	A
7.	A	17.	C	27.	D	37.	C
8.	C	18.	A	28.	A	38.	D
9.	A	19.	D	29.	C	39.	B
10.	B	20.	B	30.	C	40.	C

TEST 2

DIRECTIONS: Each question or incomplete statement is followed by several suggested answers or completions. Select the one that BEST answers the question or completes the statement. *PRINT THE LETTER OF THE CORRECT ANSWER IN THE SPACE AT THE RIGHT.*

Questions 1-5.

DIRECTIONS: Each of Questions 1 through 5 consists of a name and a dollar amount. In each question, the name and dollar amount in Column II should be an EXACT copy of the name and dollar amount in Column I. If there is:
a mistake only in the name, mark your answer A;
a mistake only in the dollar amount, mark your answer B;
a mistake in both the name and the dollar amount, mark your answer C;
no mistake in either the name or the dollar amount, mark your answer D.

SAMPLE QUESTION

Column I	Column II
George Peterson	George Petersson
$125.50	$125.50

Compare the name and dollar amount in Column II with the name and dollar amount in Column I. The name *Petersson* in Column II is spelled *Peterson* in Column I. The amount is the same in both columns. Since there is a mistake only in the name, the answer to the sample question is A. Now answer Questions 1 through 5 in the same manner.

	Column I	Column II	
1.	Susanne Shultz $3440	Susanne Schultz $3440	1.____
2.	Anibal P. Contrucci $2121.61	Anibel P. Contrucci $2112.61	2.____
3.	Eugenio Mendoza $12.45	Eugenio Mendozza $12.45	3.____
4.	Maurice Gluckstadt $4297	Maurice Gluckstadt $4297	4.____
5.	John Pampellonne $4656.94	John Pammpellonne $4566.94	5.____

Questions 6-11.

DIRECTIONS: Each of Questions 6 through 11 consist of a set of names and addresses, which you are to compare. In each question, the name and addresses in Column II should be an EXACT copy of the name and address in Column I. If there is:
    a mistake only in the name, mark your answer A;
    a mistake only in the address, mark your answer B;
    a mistake in both the name and address, mark your answer C;
    no mistake in either the name or address, mark your answer D.

SAMPLE QUESTION

Column I	Column II
Michael Filbert	Michael Filbert
456 Reade Street	645 Reade Street
New York, N.Y. 10013	New York, N.Y. 10013

Since there is a mistake only in the address (the street number should be 456 instead of 645), the answer to the sample question is B. Now answer Questions 6 through 11 in the same manner.

	Column I	Column II	
6.	Hilda Goettelmann 55 Lenox Rd. Brooklyn, N.Y. 11226	Hilda Goettelman 55 Lenox Ave. Brooklyn, N.Y. 11226	6.____
7.	Arthur Sherman 2522 Batchelder St. Brooklyn, N.Y. 11235	Arthur Sharman 2522 Batcheder St. Brooklyn, N.Y. 11253	7.____
8.	Ralph Barnett 300 West 28 Street New York, New York 10001	Ralph Barnett 300 West 28 Street New York, New York 10001	8.____
9.	George Goodwin 135 Palmer Avenue Staten Island, New York 10302	George Godwin 135 Palmer Avenue Staten Island, New York 10302	9.____
10.	Alonso Ramirez 232 West 79 Street New York, N.Y. 10024	Alonso Ramirez 223 West 79 Street New York, N.Y. 10024	10.____
11.	Cynthia Graham 149-34 83 Street Howard Beach, N.Y. 11414	Cynthia Graham 149-35 83 Street Howard Beach, N.Y. 11414	11.____

Questions 12-20.

DIRECTIONS: Questions 12 through 20 are problems in subtraction. For each question do the subtraction and select your answer from the four choices given.

12.   232,921.85
     -179,587.68

   A. 52,433.17   B. 52,434.17
   C. 53,334.17   D. 53,343,17

12.____

13.   5,531,876.29
     -3,897,158.36

   A. 1,634,717.93   B. 1,644,718.93
   C. 1,734,717.93   D. 1,7234,718.93

13.____

14.   1,482,658.22
     -937,925.76

   A. 544,633.46   B. 544,732.46
   C. 545,632.46   D. 545,732.46

14.____

15.   937,828.17
     -259,673.88

   A. 678,154.29   B. 679,154.29
   C. 688,155.39   D. 699,155.39

15.____

16.   760,412.38
     -263,465.95

   A. 496,046.43   B. 496,946.43
   C. 496,956.43   D. 497,046.43

16.____

17.   3,203,902.26
     -2,933,087.96

   A. 260,814.30   B. 269,824.30
   C. 270,814.30   D. 270,824.30

17.____

18.   1,023,468.71
     -934,678.88

   A. 88,780.83   B. 88,789.83
   C. 88,880.83   D. 88,889.83

18.____

4 (#2)

19. 831,549.47
     -772,814.78

    A. 58,734.69   B. 58,834.69
    C. 59,735.69   D. 59,834.69

19._____

20. 6,306,181.74
     -3,617,376.99

    A. 2,687,904.99   B. 2,688,904.99
    C. 2,689,804.99   D. 2,799,905.99

20._____

Questions 21-30.

DIRECTIONS: Each of Questions 21 through 30 consists of three lines of code letters and three lines of numbers. The numbers on each line should correspond with the code letters on the same line in accordance with the table below.

Code Letter	J	U	B	T	Y	D	K	R	L	P
Corresponding Number	0	1	2	3	4	5	5	7	8	9

On some of the lines, an error exists in the coding. Compare the letters and numbers in each question carefully. If you find an error or errors on:
  only *one* of the lines in the question, mark your answer A;
  any *two* lines in the question, mark your answer B;
  all *three* lines in the question, mark your answer C;
  none of the lines in the question, mark your answer D.

SAMPLE QUESTION

    BJRPYUR   2079417
    DTBPYKJ   5328460
    YKLDBLT   4685283

In the above sample, the first line is correct since each code letter listed has the correct corresponding number. On the second line, an error exists because code letter P should have the number 9 instead of the number 8. The third line is correct since each code letter listed has the correct corresponding number. Since there is an error in *one* of the three lines, the correct answer is A. Now answer Questions 21 through 30 in the same manner.

21. BYPDTJL   2495308
     PLRDTJU   9815301
     DTJRYLK   5207486

21._____

22. RPBYRJK   7934706
     PKTYLBU   9624821
     KDLPJYR   6489047

22._____

5 (#2)

23. TPYBUJR   3942107   23._____
    BYRKPTU   2476931
    DUKPYDL   5169458

24. KBYDLPL   6345898   24._____
    BLRKBRU   2876261
    JTULDYB   0318542

25. LDPYDKR   8594567   25._____
    BDKDRJL   2565708
    BDRPLUJ   2679810

26. PLRLBPU   9858291   26._____
    LPYKRDJ   88936750
    TDKPDTR   3569527

27. RKURPBY   7617924   27._____
    RYUKPTJ   7426930
    RTKPTJD   7369305

28. DYKPBJT   5469203   28._____
    KLPJBTL   6890238
    TKPLBJP   3698209

29. BTPRJYL   2397148   29._____
    LDKUTYR   8561347
    YDBLRPJ   4528190

30. ULPBKYT   1892643   30._____
    KPDTRBJ   6953720
    YLKJPTB   4860932

KEY (CORRECT ANSWERS)

1.	A	11.	D	21.	B
2.	C	12.	C	22.	C
3.	A	13.	A	23.	D
4.	D	14.	B	24.	B
5.	C	15.	A	25.	A
6.	C	16.	B	26.	C
7.	C	17.	C	27.	A
8.	D	18.	B	28.	D
9.	A	19.	A	29.	B
10.	B	20.	B	30.	D

CODING

EXAMINATION SECTION

COMMENTARY

An ingenious question-type called coding, involving elements of alphabetizing, filing, name and number comparison, and evaluative judgment and application, has currently won wide acceptance in testing circles for measuring clerical aptitude and general ability, particularly on the senior (middle) grades (levels).

While the directions for this question usually vary in detail, the candidate is generally asked to consider groups of names, codes, and numbers, and then, according to a given plan, to arrange codes in alphabetic order; to arrange these in numerical sequence; to re-arrange columns of names and numbers in correct order; to espy errors in coding; to choose the correct coding arrangement in consonance with the given directions and examples, etc.

This question-type appear to have few parameters in respect to form, substance, or degree of difficulty.

Accordingly, acquaintance with, and practice in, the coding question is recommended for the serious candidate.

TEST 1

DIRECTIONS: Questions 1 through 8 are to be answered on the basis of the code table and the instructions given below.

Code Letter for Traffic Problem	B	H	Q	J	F	L	M	I
Code Number for Action Taken	1	2	3	4	5	6	7	8

Assume that each of the capital letters on the above chart is a radio code for a particular traffic problem and that the number immediately below each capital letter is the radio code for the correct action to be taken to deal with the problem. For instance, "1" is the action to be taken to deal with problem "B", "2" is the action to be taken to deal with problem "H", and so forth.

In each question, a series of code letters is given in Column 1. Column 2 gives four different arrangements of code numbers. You are to pick the answer (A, B, C, or D) in Column 2 that gives the code numbers that match the code letters in the same order.

SAMPLE QUESTION

Column 1
BHLFMQ

Column 2
A. 125678
B. 216573
C. 127653
D. 126573

According to the chart, the code numbers that correspond to these code letters are as follows: B – 1, M – 2, L – 6, F – 5, M – 7, Q – 3. Therefore, the right answer is 126573. This answer is D in Column 2.

2 (#1)

	Column 1	Column 2	

1. BHQLMI
   - A. 123456
   - B. 123567
   - C. 123678
   - D. 125678

   1.____

2. HBJQLF
   - A. 214365
   - B. 213456
   - C. 213465
   - D. 214387

   2.____

3. QHMLFJ
   - A. 321654
   - B. 345678
   - C. 327645
   - D. 327654

   3.____

4. FLQJIM
   - A. 543287
   - B. 563487
   - C. 564378
   - D. 654378

   4.____

5. FBIHMJ
   - A. 518274
   - B. 152874
   - C. 528164
   - D. 517842

   5.____

6. MIHFQB
   - A. 872341
   - B. 782531
   - C. 782341
   - D. 783214

   6.____

7. JLFHQIM
   - A. 465237
   - B. 456387
   - C. 4652387
   - D. 4562387

   7.____

8. LBJQIFH
   - A. 614382
   - B. 6134852
   - C. 61437852
   - D. 61431852

   8.____

KEY (CORRECT ANSWERS)

1. C   5. A
2. A   6. B
3. D   7. C
4. B   8. A

TEST 2

DIRECTIONS: Each question or incomplete statement is followed by several suggested answers or completions. Select the one that BEST answers the question or completes the statement. *PRINT THE LETTER OF THE CORRECT ANSWER IN THE SPACE AT THE RIGHT.*

Questions 1-5.

DIRECTIONS: Questions 1 through 5 are based on the following list showing the name and number of each of nine inmates.

1. Johnson   4. Thompson   7. Gordon
2. Smith   5. Frank   8. Porter
3. Edwards   6. Murray   9. Lopez

Each question consists of 3 sets of numbers and letters. Each set should consist of the numbers of three inmates and the first letter of each of their names. The letters should be in the same order as the numbers. In at least two of the three choices, there will be an error. On your answer sheet, mark only that choice in which the letters correspond with the numbers and are in the same order. If all three sets are wrong, mark choice D in your answer space.

SAMPLE QUESTION
A. 386 EPM
B. 542 FST
C. 474 LGT

Since 3 corresponds to E for Edwards, 8 corresponds to P for Porter, and 6 corresponds to M for Murray, choice A is correct and should be entered in your answer space. Choice B is wrong because letters T and S have been reversed. Choice C is wrong because the first number, which is 4, does NOT correspond with the first letter of choice C, which is L. It should have been T. If choice A were also wrong, then D would be the correct answer.

1. A. 382 EGS   B. 461 TMJ   C. 875 PLF   1._____
2. A. 549 FLT   B. 692 MJS   C. 758 GSP   2._____
3. A. 936 LEM   B. 253 FSE   C. 147 JTL   3._____
4. A. 569 PML   B. 716 GJP   C. 842 PTS   4._____
5. A. 356 FEM   B. 198 JPL   C. 637 MEG   5._____

Questions 6-10.

DIRECTIONS: Questions 6 through 10 are to be answered on the basis of the following information:

2 (#3)

In order to make sure stock is properly located, incoming units are stored as follows:

STOCK NUMBERS	BIN NUMBERS
00100 – 39999	D30, L44
40000 – 69999	14L, D38
70000 – 99999	41L, 80D
100000 and over	614, 83D

Using the above table, choose the answer A, B, C, or D, which lists the correct Bin Number for the Stock Number given.

6. 17243
   A. 41L   B. 83D   C. 14L   D. D30   6.____

7. 9219
   A. D38   B. L44   C. 614   D. 41L   7.____

8. 90125
   A. 41L   B. 614   C. D38   D. D30   8.____

9. 10001
   A. L44   B. D38   C. 80D   D. 83D   9.____

10. 200100
   A. 41L   B. 14L   C. 83D   D. D30   10.____

KEY (CORRECT ANSWERS)

1.	B	6.	D
2.	D	7.	B
3.	A	8.	A
4.	C	9.	A
5.	C	10.	C

TEST 3

DIRECTIONS: Each question or incomplete statement is followed by several suggested answers or completions. Select the one that BEST answers the question or completes the statement. *PRINT THE LETTER OF THE CORRECT ANSWER IN THE SPACE AT THE RIGHT.*

Questions 1-9.

DIRECTIONS: Assume that the Police Department is planning to conduct a statistical study of individuals who have been convicted of crimes during a certain year. For the purpose of this study, identification numbers are being assigned to individuals in the following manner:

The first two digits indicate the age of the individual.
The third digit indicates the sex of the individual:
   1. Male
   2. Female
The fourth digit indicates the type of crime involved:
   1. criminal homicide
   2. forcible rape
   3. robbery
   4. aggravated assault
   5. burglary
   6. larceny
   7. auto theft
   8. other
The fifth and sixth digits indicate the month in which the conviction occurred:
   01. January
   02. February, etc.

Questions 1 through 9 are to be answered SOLELY on the basis of the above information and the following list of individuals and identification numbers.

Abbott, Richard	271304	Morris, Chris	212705
Collins, Terry	352111	Owens, William	231412
Elders, Edward	191207	Parker, Leonard	291807
George, Linda	182809	Robinson, Charles	311102
Hill, Leslie	251702	Sands, Jean	202610
Jones, Jackie	301106	Smith, Michael	42108
Lewis, Edith	402406	Turner, Donald	191601
Mack, Helen	332509	White, Barbara	242803

1. The number of women on the above list is   1.____
   A. 6   B. 7   C. 8   D. 9

2. The two convictions which occurred during February were for the crimes of
   A. aggravated assault and auto theft
   B. auto theft and criminal homicide
   C. burglary and larceny
   D. forcible rape and robbery

2._____

3. The ONLY man convicted of auto theft was
   A. Richard Abbott   B. Leslie Hill
   C. Chris Morris   D. Leonard Parker

3._____

4. The number of people on the list who were 25 years old or older is
   A. 6   B. 7   C. 8   D. 9

4._____

5. The OLDEST person on the list is
   A. Terry Collins   B. Edith Lewis
   C. Helen Mack   D. Michael Smith

5._____

6. The two people on the list who are the same age are
   A. Richard Abbott and Michael Smith
   B. Edward Elders and Donald Turner
   C. Linda George and Helen Mack
   D. Leslie Hill and Charles Robinson

6._____

7. A 28-year-old man who was convicted of aggravated assault in October would have identification number
   A. 281410   B. 281509   C. 282311   D. 282409

7._____

8. A 33-year-old woman convicted in April of criminal homicide would have identification number
   A. 331140   B. 331204   C. 332014   D. 332104

8._____

9. The number of people on the above list who were convicted during the first six months of the year is
   A. 6   B. 7   C. 8   D. 9

9._____

Questions 10-19.

DIRECTIONS: The following is a list of patients who were referred by various clinics to the laboratory for tests. After each name is a patient identification number. Questions 10 through 19 are to be answered on the basis of the information contained in this list and the explanation accompanying it.

The first digit refers to the clinic which made the referral:
1. cardiac
2. Renal
3. Pediatrics
4. Ophthalmology
5. Orthopedics
6. Hematology
7. Gynecology
8. Neurology
9. Gastroenterology

3 (#2)

The second digit refers to the sex of the patient:
1. male
2. female

The third and fourth digits give the age of the patient
The last two digits give the day of the month the laboratory tests were performed

LABORATORY REFERRALS DURING JANUARY

Adams, Jacqueline	320917	Miller, Michael	511806
Black, Leslie	813406	Pratt, William	214411
Cook, Marie	511616	Rogers, Ellen	722428
Fisher, Pat	914625	Saunders, Sally	310229
Jackson, Lee	923212	Wilson, Jan	416715
James, Linda	624621	Wyatt, Mark	321326
Lane, Arthur	115702		

10. According to the list, the number of women referred to the laboratory during January was
    A. 4 B. 5 C. 6 D. 7

11. The clinic from which the MOST patients were referred was
    A. Cardiac B. Gynecology
    C. Ophthalmology D. Pediatrics

12. The YOUNGEST patient referred from any clinic other than Pediatrics was
    A. Leslie Black B. Marie Cook
    C. Arthur Lane D. Sally Saunders

13. The number of patients whose laboratory tests were performed on or before January 16 was
    A. 7 B. 8 C. 9 D. 10

14. The number of patients referred for laboratory tests who are under age 45 is
    A. 7 B. 8 C. 9 D. 10

15. The OLDEST patient referred to the clinic during January was
    A. Jacqueline Adams B. Linda James
    C. Arthur Lane D. Jan Wilson

16. The ONLY patient treated in the Orthopedics clinic was
    A. Marie Cook B. Pat Fisher
    C. Ellen Rogers D. Jan Wilson

17. A woman, age 37 was referred from the Hematology clinic to the laboratory. Her laboratory tests were performed on January 9.
    Her identification number would be
    A. 610937 B. 623709 C. 613790 D. 623790

18. A man was referred for lab tests from the Orthopedics clinic. He is 30 years old and his tests were performed on January 6.
His identification number would be
A. 413006   B. 510360   C. 513006   D. 513060

18.____

19. A 4-year-old boy was referred from the Pediatrics clinic to have laboratory tests on January 23.
His identification number was
A. 310422   B. 310423   C. 310433   D. 320403

19.____

KEY (CORRECT ANSWERS)

1.	B	11.	D
2.	B	12.	B
3.	B	13.	A
4.	D	14.	C
5.	D	15.	D
6.	B	16.	A
7.	A	17.	B
8.	D	18.	C
9.	C	19.	B
10.	B		

TEST 4

DIRECTIONS: Each question or incomplete statement is followed by several suggested answers or completions. Select the one that BEST answers the question or completes the statement. *PRINT THE LETTER OF THE CORRECT ANSWER IN THE SPACE AT THE RIGHT.*

Questions 1-10.

DIRECTIONS: Questions 1 through 10 are to be answered on the basis of the information and directions given below.

Assume that you are a Senior Stenographer assigned to the personnel bureau of a city agency. Your supervisor has asked you to classify the employees in your agency into the following five groups:

- A. Employees who are college graduates, who are at least 35 years of age but less than 50, and who have been employed by the City for five years or more;
- B. Employees who have been employed by the City for less than five years, who are not college graduates, and who earn at least $32,500 a year but less than $34,500;
- C. Employees who have been City employees for five years or more, who are at least 21 years of age but less than 35, and who are not college graduates;
- D. Employee who earn at least $34,500 a year but less than $36,000 who are college graduates, and who have been employed by the City for less than five years;
- E. Employees who are not included in any of the foregoing groups.

NOTE: In classifying these employees you are to compute age and period of service as of January 1, 2003. In all cases, it is to be assumed that each employee has been employed continuously in City service. In each question, consider only the information which will assist you in classifying each employee Any information which is of no assistance in classifying an employee would not be considered.

SAMPLE: Mr. Brown, a 29-year-old veteran, was appointed to his present position of Clerk on June 1, 2000. He has completed two years of college. His present salary is $33,050.

The correct answer to this sample is B, since the employee has been employed by the City for less than five years, is not a college graduate, and earn at least $32,500 a year but less than $34,500.

Questions 1 through 10 contain excerpts from the personnel records of 10 employees in the agency. In the correspondingly numbered space at the right print the capital letter preceding the appropriate group into which you would place each employee.

1. Mr. James has been employed by the City since 1993, when he was graduated from a local college. Now 35 years of age, he earns $36,000 a year.   1.____

2. Mr. Worth began working in City service early in 1999. He was awarded his college degree in 1994, at the age of 21. As a result of a recent promotion, he now earns $34,500 a year.   2.____

2 (#4)

3. Miss Thomas has been a City employee since August 1, 1998. Her salary is $34,500 a year. Miss Thomas, who is 25 years old, has had only three years of high school training.

3._____

4. Mr. Williams has had three promotions since entering City service on January 1, 1991. He was graduated from college with honors in 1974, when he was 20 years of age. His present salary is $37,000 a year.

4._____

5. Miss Jones left college after two years of study to take an appointment to a position in the City service paying $33,300 a year. She began work on March 1, 1997 when she was 19 years of age.

5._____

6. Mr. Smith was graduated from an engineering college with honors in January 1998 and became a City employee three months later. His present salary is $35,810. Mr. Smith was born in 1976.

6._____

7. Miss Earnest was born on May 31, 1979. Her education consisted of four years of high school and one year of business school. She was appointed as a typist in a City agency on June 1, 1997. Her annual salary is $33,500.

7._____

8. Mr. Adams, a 24-year-old clerk, began his City service on July 1, 1999, soon after being discharged from the U.S. Army. A college graduate, his present annual salary is $33,200.

8._____

9. Miss Charles attends college in the evenings, hoping to obtain her degree is 2004, when she will be 30 years of age. She has been a City employee since April 1998, and earns $33,350.

9._____

10. Mr. Dolan was just promoted to his present position after six years of City service. He was graduated from high school in 1982, when he was 18 years of age, but did not go on to college. Mr. Dolan's present salary is $33,500.

10._____

KEY (CORRECT ANSWERS)

1. A   6. D
2. D   7. C
3. E   8. E
4. A   9. B
5. C   10. E

TEST 5

DIRECTIONS: Questions 1 through 4 each contain five numbers that should be arranged in numerical order. The number with the lowest numerical value should be first and the number with the highest numerical value should be last. Pick that option which indicates the CORRECT order of the numbers.

Examples: A. 9; 18; 14; 15; 27
B. 9; 14; 15; 18; 27
C. 14; 15; 18; 27; 9
D. 9; 14; 15; 27; 18

The correct answer is B, which contains the proper arrangement of the five numbers.

1. A. 20573; 20753; 20738; 20837; 20098
   B. 20098; 20753; 20573; 20738; 20837
   C. 20098; 20573; 20753; 20837; 20738
   D. 20098; 20573; 20738; 20753; 20837

2. A. 113492; 113429; 111314; 113114; 131413
   B. 111314; 113114; 113429; 113492; 131413
   C. 111314; 113429; 113492; 113114; 131413
   D. 111314; 113114; 131413; 113429; 113492

3. A. 1029763; 1030421; 1035681; 1036928; 1067391
   B. 1030421; 1029763; 1035681; 1067391; 1036928
   C. 1030421; 1035681; 1036928; 1067391; 1029763
   D. 1029763; 1039421; 1035681; 1067391; 1036928

4. A. 1112315; 1112326; 1112337; 1112349; 1112306
   B. 1112306; 1112315; 1112337; 1112326; 1112349
   C. 1112306; 1112315; 1112326; 1112337; 1112349
   D. 1112306; 1112326; 1112315; 1112337; 1112349

1.____
2.____
3.____
4.____

KEY (CORRECT ANSWERS)

1. D
2. B
3. A
4. C

TEST 6

DIRECTIONS: The phonetic filing system is a method of filing names in which the alphabet is reduced to key code letters. The six key letters and their equivalents are as follows:

KEY LETTERS	EQUIVALENTS
b	p, f, v
c	s, k, g, j, q, x, z
d	t
l	none
m	n
r	none

A key letter represents itself.
Vowels (a, e, i, o, and u) and the letters w, h, and y are omitted.
For example, the name GILMAN would be represented as follows:
 G is represented by the key letter C.
 I is a vowel and is omitted.
 L is a letter and represents itself.
 M is a key letter and represents itself.
 A is a vowel and is omitted.
 N is represented by the key letter M.

Therefore, the phonetic filing code for the name GILMAN is CLMM.

Answer Questions 1 through 10 based on the information below.

1. The phonetic filing code for the name FITZGERALD would be
   A. BDCCRLD   B. BDCRLD   C. BDZCRLD   D. BTZCRLD

2. The phonetic filing code CLBR may represent any one of the following names EXCEPT
   A. Calprey   B. Flower   C. Glover   D. Silver

3. The phonetic filing code LDM may represent any one of the following names EXCEPT
   A. Halden   B. Hilton   C. Walton   D. Wilson

4. The phonetic filing code for the name RODRIGUEZ would be
   A. RDRC   B. RDRCC   C. RDRCZ   D. RTRCC

5. The phonetic filing code for the name MAXWELL would be
   A. MCLL   B. MCWL   C. MCWLL   D. MXLL

6. The phonetic filing code for the name ANDERSON would be
   A. AMDRCM   B. ENDRSM   C. MDRCM   D. NDERCN

7. The phonetic filing code for the name SAVITSKY would be
   A. CBDCC   B. CBDCY   C. SBDCC   D. SVDCC

8. The phonetic filing code CMC may represent any one of the following names EXCEPT 8._____
   A. James B. Jayes C. Johns D. Jones

9. The ONLY one of the following names that could be represented by the phonetic filing code CDDDM would be 9._____
   A. Catalano B. Chesterton C. Cittadino D. Cuttlerman

10. The ONLY one of the following names that could be represented by the phonetic filing code LLMCM would be 10._____
    A. Ellington B. Hallerman C. Inslerman D. Willingham

KEY (CORRECT ANSWERS)

1.	A	6.	C
2.	B	7.	A
3.	D	8.	B
4.	B	9.	C
5.	A	10.	D

NAME AND NUMBER CHECKING
EXAMINATION SECTION
TEST 1

DIRECTIONS: This test is designed to measure your speed/and accuracy. You are urged to work both quickly and accurately and to do correctly as many lists as you can in the time allowed. The test consists of lists or pairs of names and numbers. Count the number of IDENTICAL pairs in each list. Then, select the correct number, 1, 2, 3, 4, 5, and indicate your choice in the space at the right. Two sample questions are presented for your guidance, together with the correct solutions.

SAMPLE LIST A
Adelphi College – Adelphia College
Braxton Corp – Braxeton Corp.
Wassaic State School – Wassaic State School
Central Islip State Hospital – Central Isllip State Hospital
Greenwich House – Greenwich House

NOTE: There are only two correct pairs—Wassaic State School and Greenwich House. Therefore, the CORRECT answer is 2.

SAMPLE LIST B
78453694 – 78453684
784530 – 784530
533 – 534
67845 – 67845
2368745 – 2368755

NOTE: There are only two correct pairs—784530 and 67845. Therefore, the CORRECT answer is 2.

LIST 1
    Diagnostic Clinic   – Diagnostic Clinic
    Yorkville Health   – Yorkville Health
    Meinhard Clinic   – Meinhart Clinic
    Corlears Clinic   – Carlears Clinic
    Tremont Diagnostic   – Tremont Diagnostic

1.____

LIST 2
    73526   – 73526
    7283627198   – 7283627198
    627   – 637
    728352617283   – 7283526178282
    6281   – 6281

2.____

2 (#1)

LIST 3 3._____
    Jefferson Clinic   – Jeffersen Clinic
    Mott Haven Center   – Mott Havan Center
    Bronx Hospital   – Bronx Hospital
    Montefiore Hospital   – Montifeore Hospital
    Beth Isreal Hospital   – Beth Israel Hospital

LIST 4 4._____
    936271826   – 936371826
    5271   – 5291
    82637192037   – 82637192037
    527182   – 5271882
    726354256   - 72635456

LIST 5 5._____
    Trinity Hospital   – Trinity Hospital
    Central Harlem   – Centrel Harlem
    St. Luke's Hospital   – St. Lukes' Hospital
    Mt. Sinai Hospital   – Mt. Sinia Hospital
    N.Y. Dispensery   – N.Y. Dispensary

LIST 6 6._____
    725361552637   – 725361555637
    7526378   – 7526377
    6975   – 6975
    82637481028   – 82637481028
    3427   – 3429

LIST 7 7._____
    Misericordia Hospital   – Miseracordia Hospital
    Lebonan Hospital   – Lebanon Hospital
    Gouverneur Hospital   – Gouverner Hospital
    German Polyclinic   – German Policlinic
    French Hospital   – French Hospital

LIST 8 8._____
    8277364933251   – 827364933351
    63728   – 63728
    367281   – 367281
    62733846273   – 6273846293
    62836   - 6283

LIST 9 9._____
    King's County Hospital   – Kings County Hospital
    St. Johns Long Island   – St. John's Long Island
    Bellevue Hospital   – Bellvue Hospital
    Beth David Hospital   – Beth David Hospital
    Samaritan Hospital   – Samariton Hospital

LIST 10
62836454	– 62836455
42738267	– 42738369
573829	– 573829
738291627874	– 738291627874
725	- 735

10.____

LIST 11
Bloomingdal Clinic	– Bloomingdale Clinic
Communitty Hospital	– Community Hospital
Metroplitan Hospital	– Metropoliton Hospital
Lenox Hill Hospital	– Lonex Hill Hospital
Lincoln Hospital	– Lincoln Hospital

11.____

LIST 12
6283364728	– 6283648
627385	– 627383
54283902	– 54283602
63354	– 63354
7283562781	- 7283562781

12.____

LIST 13
Sydenham Hospital	– Sydanham Hospital
Roosevalt Hospital	– Roosevelt Hospital
Vanderbilt Clinic	– Vanderbild Clinic
Women's Hospital	– Woman's Hospital
Flushing Hospital	– Flushing Hospital

13.____

LIST 14
62738	– 62738
727355542321	– 72735542321
263849332	– 263849332
262837	– 263837
47382912	- 47382922

14.____

LIST 15
Episcopal Hospital	– Episcapal Hospital
Flower Hospital	– Flouer Hospital
Stuyvesent Clinic	– Stuyvesant Clinic
Jamaica Clinic	– Jamaica Clinic
Ridgwood Clinic	– Ridgewood Clinic

15.____

LIST 16
628367299	– 628367399
111	– 111
118293304829	– 1182839489
4448	– 4448
333693678	- 333693678

16.____

4 (#1)

LIST 17   17.____
    Arietta Crane Farm   – Areitta Crane Farm
    Bikur Chilim Home   – Bikur Chilom Home
    Burke Foundation   – Burke Foundation
    Blythedale Home   – Blythdale Home
    Campbell Cottages   – Cambell Cottages

LIST 18   18.____
    32123   – 32132
    273893326783   – 27389326783
    473829   – 473829
    7382937   – 7383937
    3628890122332   - 36289012332

LIST 19   19.____
    Caraline Rest   – Caroline Rest
    Loreto Rest   – Loretto Rest
    Edgewater Creche   – Edgwater Creche
    Holiday Farm   – Holiday Farm
    House of St. Giles   – House of st. Giles

LIST 20   20.____
    557286777   – 55728677
    3678902   – 3678892
    1567839   – 1567839
    7865434712   – 7865344712
    9927382   - 9927382

LIST 21   21.____
    Isabella Home   – Isabela Home
    James A. Moore Home   – James A. More Home
    The Robin's Nest   – The Roben's Nest
    Pelham Home   – Pelam Home
    St. Eleanora's Home   – St. Eleanora's Home

LIST 22   22.____
    273648293048   – 273648293048
    334   – 334
    7362536478   – 7362536478
    7362819273   – 7362819273
    7362   - 7363

LIST 23   23.____
    St. Pheobe's Mission   – St. Phebe's Mission
    Seaside Home   – Seaside Home
    Speedwell Society   – Speedwell Society
    Valeria Home   – Valera Home
    Wiltwyck   - Wildwyck

5 (#1)

LIST 24
63728 — 63738
63728192736 — 63728192738
428 — 458
62738291527 — 62738291529
63728192 - 63728192

LIST 25
McGaffin — McGafin
David Ardslee — David Ardslee
Axton Supply — Axeton Supply Co
Alice Russell — Alice Russell
Dobson Mfg. Co. — Dobsen Mfg. Co.

24.____

25.____

KEY (CORRECT ANSWERS)

1.	3		11.	1
2.	3		12.	2
3.	1		13.	1
4.	1		14.	2
5.	1		15.	1
6.	2		16.	3
7.	1		17.	1
8.	2		18.	1
9.	1		19.	1
10.	2		20.	2

21. 1
22. 4
23. 2
24. 1
25. 2

TEST 2

DIRECTIONS: This test is designed to measure your speed/and accuracy. You are urged to work both quickly and accurately and to do correctly as many lists as you can in the time allowed. The test consists of lists or pairs of names and numbers. Count the number of IDENTICAL pairs in each list. Then, select the correct number, 1, 2, 3, 4, 5, and indicate your choice in the space at the right.

LIST 1
    82637381028   – 82637281028
    928   – 928
    72937281028   – 72937281028
    7362   – 7362
    927382615   – 927382615

1._____

LIST 2
    Albee Theatre   – Albee Theatre
    Lapland Lumber Co. – Laplund Lumber Co.
    Adelphi College   – Adelphi College
    Jones & Son Inc.   – Jones & Sons Inc.
    S.W. Ponds Co.   – S.W. Ponds Co.

2._____

LIST 3
    85345   – 85345
    895643278   – 895643277
    726352   – 726353
    632685   – 632685
    7263524   – 7236524

3._____

LIST 4
    Eagle Library   – Eagle Library
    Dodge Ltd.   – Dodge Co.
    Stromberg Carlson   – Stromberg Carlsen
    Clairice Ling   – Clairice Linng
    Mason Book Co.   – Matson Book Co.

4._____

LIST 5
    66273   – 66273
    629   – 629
    7382517283   – 7382517283
    637281   – 639281
    2738261   – 2788261

5._____

LIST 6
    Robert MacColl   – Robert McColl
    Buick Motor   – Buck Motors
    Murray Bay & Co. Ltd. – Murray Bay Co. Ltd.
    L.T. Ltyle   – L.T. Lyttle
    A.S. Landas   – A.S. Landas

6._____

2 (#2)

LIST 7   7.____
    6271526374890   – 627152637490
    73526189   – 73526189
    5372   – 5392
    637281142   – 63728124
    4783946   – 4783046

LIST 8   8.____
    Tyndall Burke   – Tyndell Burke
    W. Briehl   – W. Briehl
    Burritt Publishing Co. – Buritt Publishing Co.
    Frederick Breyer & Co. – Frederick Breyer Co.
    Bailey Buulard   – Bailey Bullard

LIST 9   9.____
    634   – 634
    16837   – 163837
    273892223678   – 27389223678
    527182   – 527782
    3628901223   – 3629002223

LIST 10   10.____
    Ernest Boas   – Ernest Boas
    Rankin Barne   – Rankin Barnes
    Edward Appley   – Edward Appely
    Camel   – Camel
    Caiger Food Co.   – Caiger Food Co.

LIST 11   11.____
    6273   – 6273
    322   – 332
    15672839   – 15672839
    63728192637   – 63728192639
    738   – 738

LIST 12   12.____
    Wells Fargo Co.   – Wells Fargo Co.
    W.D. Brett   – W.D. Britt
    Tassco Co.   – Tassko Co.
    Republic Mills   – Republic Mill
    R.W. Burnham   – R.W. Burhnam

LIST 13   13.____
    7253529152   – 7283529152
    6283   – 6383
    52839102738   – 5283910238
    308   – 398
    82637201927   – 8263720127

LIST 14
Schumacker Co.	– Shumacker Co.	14.____
C.H. Caiger	– C.H. Caiger	
Abraham Strauss	– Abram Straus	
B.F. Boettjer	– B.F. Boettijer	
Cut-Rate Store	– Cut-Rate Stores	

LIST 15
15273826	– 15273826	15.____
72537	– 73537	
726391027384	– 62639107384	
637389	– 627399	
725382910	– 725382910	

LIST 16
Hixby Ltd.	– Hixby Lt'd.	16.____
S. Reiner	– S. Riener	
Reynard Co.	– Reynord Co.	
Esso Gassoline Co.	– Esso Gasolene Co.	
Belle Brock	– Belle Brock	

LIST 17
7245	– 7245	17.____
819263728192	– 819263728172	
682537289	– 682537298	
789	– 789	
82936542891	– 82936542891	

LIST 18
Joseph Cartwright	– Joseph Cartwrite	18.____
Foote Food Co.	– Foot Food Co.	
Weiman & Held	– Weiman & Held	
Sanderson Shoe Co.	– Sandersen Shoe Co.	
A.M. Byrne	– A.N. Byrne	

LIST 19
4738267	– 4738277	19.____
63728	– 63729	
6283628901	– 6283628991	
918264	– 918264	
263728192037	– 2637728192073	

LIST 20
Exray Laboratories	– Exray Labratories	20.____
Curley Toy Co.	– Curly Toy Co.	
J. Lauer & Cross	– J. Laeur & Cross	
Mireco Brands	– Mireco Brands	
Sandor Lorand	– Sandor Larand	

4 (#2)

LIST 21   21._____
　607   – 609
　6405   – 6403
　976   – 996
　101267   – 101267
　2065432   – 20965432

LIST 22   22._____
　John Macy & Sons   – John Macy & Son
　Venus Pencil Co.   – Venus Pencil Co.
　Nell McGinnis   – Nell McGinnis
　McCutcheon & Co.   – McCutcheon & Co.
　Sun-Tan Oil   – Sun-Tan Oil

LIST 23   23._____
　703345700   – 703345700
　46754   – 466754
　3367490   – 3367490
　3379   – 3778
　47384   – 47394

LIST 24   24._____
　arthritis   – arthritis
　asthma   – asthma
　endocrine   – endocrene
　gastro-enterological   – gastrol-enteralogical
　orthopedic   – orthopedic

LIST 25   25._____
　743829432   – 743828432
　998   – 998
　732816253902   – 732816252902
　46829   – 46830
　7439120249   – 7439210249

145

KEY (CORRECT ANSWERS)

1.	4	11.	3
2.	3	12.	1
3.	2	13.	1
4.	1	14.	1
5.	2	15.	2
6.	1	16.	1
7.	2	17.	3
8.	1	18.	1
9.	1	19.	1
10.	3	20.	1

21.	1
22.	4
23.	2
24.	3
25.	1

POLICE SCIENCE NOTES

POLICE RECORDS

TABLE OF CONTENTS

	Page
COMMENTARY	1
FILING	1
FILING BY CLASSIFICATION AND CASE	2
STATISTICS	3
MOTOR VEHICLE ACCIDENTS	4
UNIFORM TRAFFIC TICKETS	4
JUVENILE AND YOUTH POLICE RECORDS	4

POLICE SCIENCE NOTES

POLICE RECORDS

Records are of vital importance to a law enforcement agency, whether large or small. A records system should be centralized for a law enforcement agency as a whole. Separate sets of independent records in various sections or divisions of an agency or department are less useful and less desirable than centralized records. For example, a uniformed patrolman's initial report on a store burglary and a later investigative report on the same burglary prepared by the detective assigned to a case should be filed together, rather than in separate files, in the Uniform Division and the Detective Division.

FILING

All reports, memoranda, letters, etc., should be filed with other documents relating to the same case or matter, in chronological order. By this means, the entire experience of the department in connection with any particular case or classification of cases or matters can be readily located for review and analysis, as desired. In addition, it simplifies locating reports when the names or subjects involved are unknown or have been forgotten.

In order to permit filing of reports, letters, memoranda, and other documents in a logical, usable way (i.e., burglary cases in the burglary classification files, assaults in the assault classification files, correspondence on police uniforms with similar correspondence, in the "uniforms" classification file, etc.), it is necessary to assign classifications to reports and other documents to be filed. In order to do so, a list of "file classifications" and "file classification numbers" must be prepared and used. The classification list of each department will depend on size, specific needs, and on the variety of classifications assigned to administrative things (all police departments should have approximately the same classifications for crimes, since all are governed by the same law).

A usable classification system, for example, could begin with classifications such as: 1 - Applicant, 2 – Alcoholic Beverage Control Law, 3 – Abandonment, 4 – Accidents, etc. The system should segregate crimes into classifications by kind of crime.

Each report, memorandum, letter or document to be filed should be assigned an unvarying classification number (e.g., anything to do with an abortion case would be marked "3"), followed by the number assigned the particular case or matter, and, if desired, a serial number.

Thus, a uniformed officer's report from an informant concerning child abandonment by a Mr. X, which would begin a new case, would be marked (on the first page only, usually at lower right) with "3" for the classification abandonment followed by a dash and a number following the number of the last case in file (e.g., "3-42").

If serial numbering is desired, the report would be marked "3-42-1". The next document filed would be "3-42-2," etc. The "1" shows the report is the first document put in file 3-42.

Files, of course, may be kept loose in individually numbered folders, or as documents permanently put together with patent fasteners of various kinds, or in files with covers, without covers, etc. A secure method should be adopted and used uniformly.

Where a classification system is used, it permits clerical filing "by the numbers" with accuracy, insuring that (for example) all abandonment cases and correspondence or other material relating to them not only go in the same place in files, but that pieces of a particular case are filed in proper order with the case and not someplace else where they have to be hunted and may be lost. Procedure should be the same for any classification, whether it is "ABC Law," "Supply of Uniforms," "Vehicle Maintenance," or anything else.

FILING BY CLASSIFICATION AND CASE

Reports, letters, memoranda, and other documents should be identified, for filing and finding, by classification, file and serial number, in that order (e.g., 3-42-1).

1. Classification Number: The first digit or digits of a complete "file number." It identifies the classification. In the example given, the classification number "3" indicates the case reported relates to abandonment.

2. Case Number: The second digit or digits of the file number. It identifies the particular case concerned. Case numbers should be assigned consecutively (to initial reports or documents of cases in the same classification as they are received). Once a case has been assigned a case number, all reports in that case should carry the same number. In the example given, the number 42 indicates that the case is the 42nd case report in this particular classification.

   Each classification should also have a zero (0) case file and a double zero (00) case file.

   a. Zero (0) Case File: The zero case file should contain material of a non-specific nature which relates to a particular classification but does not relate to any particular case in the classification. This will be material on which no cases need be opened.

   b. Double Zero (00) File: A double zero file should be used solely for rules and instructions relating to the particular classification (not pertaining to any specific case but to the classification generally).

3. Serial Number: A serial number indicates the order in which the report or other document was received in relation to other reports or documents in the same case file. Serial numbers should be assigned consecutively, as the material is received for filing. They permit permanent accounting for all items in file.

Reports should be classified and assigned their classification and case numbers as they are received. Reports should, of course, be reviewed by supervisory personnel for content, errors, etc. When corrections are required, they should be brought to the attention of the responsible officer for appropriate action. If a report is satisfactory, it may then be indexed, given a serial number, and filed.

Files in each classification should be kept in numerical order, behind a divider which identifies the classification.

In the file room, names of the title or heading of the first report or document filed should be indexed. Thereafter, only changes or additions need be indexed. Any other names which appear in an investigation or document which are desirable to index, should be underlined by the officer or reviewing supervisor (on file copy) in red ink or pencil, with a red check mark on the first page of the report as a flag to file room personnel that there is indexing required. Supervisors should be alert to ensure that all necessary indexing is marked on file copies before they are sent to the file room. The index cards in all instances must show the name of the person or item, and the file number (classification and case numbers). Brief identifying data may also be entered (e.g., "fem, born 8/12/61").

In cases where there are any exhibits or evidence in file which are not to be retained as a permanent part of the case, a report should be placed in file showing the final disposition of them. Supervisors should ensure that evidence and exhibits are promptly disposed of when they have served their purpose. Appropriate receipts should be obtained when property is disposed of by means other than by destruction.

STATISTICS

All police agencies maintain certain crime and arrest statistics covering their jurisdiction. They must submit these statistics to the Department every calendar month on forms supplied by the Department. No police agency is exempted by reason of its size or lack of personnel.

Statistics are required concerning felonies, misdemeanors, and other offenses and on all persons arrested for such crimes and offenses, as specified by the Department in its statistical forms.

The statistics must show the number of offenses known to the police, how many were determined to be unfounded, and how many were "cleared by arrest." The data on arrested persons must include the county of arrest, the specific crime or offense charged, their sex, and their age. Forms and instructions may be secured directly from the Department of Corrections.

The Federal Bureau of Investigation, U.S. Department of Justice, Washington, D.C., also collects crime statistics on a monthly basis, for the national Uniform Crime Reports. Police agencies not contributing should consider doing so. Necessary details, instructions, and forms may be secured by writing to the Director, Federal Bureau of Investigation, U.S. Department of Justice, Washington, D.C., or by contacting the nearest F.B.I. office.

In order to comply with state law and to provide the basic minimum records necessary, even the smallest department must maintain a record of complaints received and a notation of action taken thereon. It must also maintain a record of persons arrested.

Such records may be maintained in their simplest form in a "blotter" or other bound volume. They are better and more useful on a separate form for each complaint and for each arrest. Separate forms may be filed in separate files by case and by classification, for various administrative uses and analyses. Such an arrangement is a bare minimum. Departments desiring to establish new and better record systems or to alter and improve old ones may obtain a "Manual of Police Records" from the Director, Federal Bureau of Investigation, U.S. Department of Justice, Washington, D.C., free of charge.

Data entered on complaint forms should always include notation as to the action taken, by whom taken, and the final disposition of the matter.

MOTOR VEHICLE ACCIDENTS

The Vehicle and Traffic Law requires all officers to investigate every motor vehicle involving a personal injury which is reported to them within five days after the accident. They must make a report of their investigation to the Commissioner of Motor Vehicles on forms furnished by the Department of Motor Vehicles.

All reports and records of any accident (not alone motor vehicle) which are kept by the State Police or by the police force of any county, city, town, or village or other district of the State, shall be open to the inspection of any person having an interest therein or his attorney or agent, except that any report or reports may be withheld from inspection if their disclosure would interfere with the investigation or prosecution of a crime involved in or connected with the accident. All departments, therefore, must keep their accident files in proper order, so that the reports may be readily located when required. This may be done by numbering and indexing or by filing by place and date of accident.

UNIFORM TRAFFIC TICKETS

Under the Vehicle and Traffic Law and the Regulations of the Commissioner of Motor Vehicles, all police must use the prescribed Uniform Traffic Ticket. In addition, they are required to maintain a file of Part IV of the uniform ticket. This is one of the copies delivered to the court by the issuing officer; on it the court notes the disposition and forwards it to the department of the issuing officer.

JUVENILE AND YOUTH POLICE RECORDS

All records of police relating to juvenile delinquents, persons in need of supervision or youthful offenders must be kept confidential. They may, however, be inspected upon order from the court wherein the subject was adjudged, or, without a court order, by the institution to which a youth has been committed.

Juvenile Delinquency and Persons in Need of Supervision police records must be kept by police in files separate and apart from similar files on adults. Youthful Offender files need not be separately maintained by police.

www.ingramcontent.com/pod-product-compliance
Lightning Source LLC
Chambersburg PA
CBHW080324020526

44117CB00035B/2642